National Curriculum Standards for Social Studies

I Culture

Social studies programs should include experiences that provide for the study of culture and cultural diversity.

II Time, Continuity, & Change

Social studies programs should include experiences that provide for the study of the ways human beings view themselves in and over time while recognizing examples of change and cause and effect relationships.

iii People, Places, & Environments

Social studies programs should include experiences that provide for the study of people, places, and environments.

IV Individual Development & Identity

Social studies programs should include experiences that provide for the study of individual development and identity while recognizing personal changes over time and personal connections to places.

V Individuals, Groups, & Institutions

Social studies programs should include experiences that provide for the study of interactions among individuals, groups, and institutions while giving examples of and explaining, group and institutional influences on people, events, and elements of culture.

VI Power, Authority, & Governance

Social studies programs should include experiences that provide for the study of how people create and change structures of power, authority, and governance while examining the rights and responsibilities of the individual in relation to his or her social group.

VII Production, Distribution, & Consumption

Social studies programs should include experiences that provide for the study of how people organize for the production, distribution, and consumption of goods and services.

VIII Science, Technology, & Society

Social studies programs should include experiences that provide for the study of relationships among science, technology, and society.

IX Global Connections

Social studies programs should include experiences that provide for the study of global connections and independence while giving examples of conflict, cooperation, and interdependence among individuals, groups, and nations.

X Civic Ideals & Practices

Social studies programs should include experiences that provide for the study of the ideals, principles, and practices of citizenship in a democratic republic.

National Geography Standards

The *Geographically Informed Person* knows and understands . . .

THE WORLD IN SPATIAL TERMS

STANDARD 1: How to use maps and other geographic representations, tools, and technologies to acquire, process, and report information.

STANDARD 2: How to use mental maps to organize information about people, places, and environments.

STANDARD 3: How to analyze the spatial organization of people, places, and environments on Earth's surface.

PLACES AND REGIONS

STANDARD 4: The physical and human characteristics of places.

STANDARD 5: That people create regions to interpret Earth's complexity.

STANDARD 6: How culture and experience influence people's perception of places and regions.

PHYSICAL SYSTEMS

STANDARD 7: The physical processes that shape the patterns of Earth's surface.

STANDARD 8: The characteristics and spatial distribution of ecosystems on Earth's surface.

HUMAN SYSTEMS

STANDARD 9: The characteristics, distribution, and migration of human populations on Earth's surface.

STANDARD 10: The characteristics, distributions, and complexity of Earth's cultural mosaics.

STANDARD 11: The patterns and networks of economic interdependence on Earth's surface.

STANDARD 12: The process, patterns, and functions of human settlement.

STANDARD 13: How forces of cooperation and conflict among people influence the division and control of Earth's surface.

ENVIRONMENT AND SOCIETY

STANDARD 14: How human actions modify the physical environment.

STANDARD 15: How physical systems affect human systems.

STANDARD 16: The changes that occur in the meaning, use, distribution, and importance of resources.

THE USES OF GEOGRAPHY

STANDARD 17: How to apply geography to interpret the past.

STANDARD 18: To apply geography to interpret the present and plan for the future.

Macmillan/McGraw-Hill TimeLinks

Communities

PROGRAM AUTHORS

James A. Banks
Kevin P. Colleary
Linda Greenow
Walter C. Parker
Emily M. Schell
Dinah Zike

CONTRIBUTORS

Raymond C. Jones
Irma M. Olmedo

Macmillan/McGraw-Hill

PROGRAM AUTHORS

James A. Banks, Ph.D.
Kerry and Linda Killinger Professor
  of Diversity Studies
  and Director, Center for
  Multicultural Education
University of Washington
Seattle, Washington

Kevin P. Colleary, Ed.D.
Curriculum and Teaching Department
Graduate School of Education
Fordham University
New York, New York

Linda Greenow, Ph.D.
Associate Professor and Chair
Department of Geography
State University of New York at New Paltz
New Paltz, New York

Walter C. Parker, Ph.D.
Professor of Social Studies Education,
  Adjunct Professor of Political Science
University of Washington
Seattle, Washington

Emily M. Schell, Ed.D.
Visiting Professor, Teacher Education
San Diego State University
San Diego, California

Dinah Zike
Educational Consultant
Dinah-Mite Activities, Inc.
San Antonio, Texas

CONTRIBUTORS

Raymond C. Jones, Ph.D.
Director of Secondary Social Studies
  Education
Wake Forest University
Winston-Salem, North Carolina

Irma M. Olmedo
Associate Professor
University of Illinois-Chicago
College of Education
Chicago, Illinois

HISTORIANS/SCHOLARS

Thomas Bender, Ph.D.
Professor of History
New York University
New York, New York

Ned Blackhawk
Associate Professor of History
  and American Indian Studies
University of Wisconsin
Madison, Wisconsin

Manuel Chavez, Ph.D.
Associate Director, Center for
  Latin American & Caribbean Studies
Assistant Professor, School of Journalism
Michigan State University
East Lansing, Michigan

Sheilah F. Clarke-Ekong, Ph.D.
Professor of Anthropology
University of Missouri-St. Louis
St. Louis, Missouri

Larry Dale, Ph.D.
Director, Center for Economic Education
Arkansas State University
Jonesboro, Arkansas

Brooks Green, Ph.D.
Associate Professor of Geography
University of Central Arkansas
Conway, Arkansas

Thomas C. Holt, Ph.D.
Professor of History
University of Chicago
Chicago, Illinois

Paula Kluth, Ph.D.
Independent Scholar
  and Special Education Consultant
Oak Park, Illinois

Andrei V. Korobkov, Ph.D.
Associate Professor
Department of Political Science
Middle Tennessee State University
Murfreesboro, Tennessee

Nayanjot Lahiri
Professor, Department of History
University of Delhi
Delhi, India

Mac Dixon-Fyle, Ph.D.
Professor of History
DePauw University
Greencastle, Indiana

Oscar J. Martinez, Ph.D.
Regents Professor of History
University of Arizona
Tucson, Arizona

Students with print disabilities may be eligible to obtain an accessible, audio version of the pupil edition of this textbook. Please call Recording for the Blind & Dyslexic at 1-800-221-4792 for complete information.

The **McGraw-Hill** Companies

Macmillan McGraw-Hill

MHID 0-02-151346-5

ISBN 978-0-02-151346-8

Printed in the United States of America

6 7 8 9 10   QDB/LEH   13 12

Communities
CONTENTS

Unit 2 Communities Change 49

How do communities change over time?

v

Reference Section

Maps

Skills and Features

Unit 1

EXPLORE The Big Idea

Essential Question
How does where you live affect how you live?

FOLDABLES™
Study Organizer

Main Idea and Details
Use a concept map foldable to take notes as you read Unit 1.

Label the sections **Community Size**, **Resources**, and **Climate**. Use the foldable to organize information as you read the unit.

Where You Live

| Community Size | Resources | Climate |

LOG ON **For more about Unit 1 go to**
www.macmillanmh.com

Pittsburgh, Pennsylvania

Communities and Geography

1

PEOPLE, PLACES, AND EVENTS

Senator Gaylord Nelson

Earth Day Groceries Project in Illinois

Save THE Earth!

Earth Day

1970
At a meeting in Seattle, Washington, Senator Nelson announced plans for the first Earth Day.

On April 22, 1970, **Senator Gaylord Nelson** announced plans for the first **Earth Day** celebration.

Today students in **Illinois** and elsewhere take part in the Earth Day Groceries Project.

For more about People, Places, and Events, visit
www.macmillanmh.com

Lord Norman Foster

Hearst Tower in
New York City

Building a "Green Building"

2005 Hearst Tower is a "green building." That means it was built to save energy.

Lord Norman Foster designed the **Hearst Tower in New York City** to be a "**green building**."

Today you can visit Hearst Tower and see what makes it green!

3

What Is a Community?

Lesson 1

VOCABULARY
community p. 5

geography p. 5

capital p. 6

festival p. 7

READING SKILL
Main Idea and Details
Copy the chart below. As you read, fill it in with ideas and details about people who live, work, and play in Raleigh.

Main Idea	Details

STANDARDS FOCUS

SOCIAL STUDIES Individuals, Groups, and Institutions

GEOGRAPHY Human Systems

Street festival
Raleigh, North Carolina

Visual Preview

What makes a community?

A Communities are where people live, work, and play.

B People in a community work at many kinds of jobs.

C People in many communities help one another.

THINK ABOUT COMMUNITIES

Raleigh is a city in North Carolina. The people of Raleigh think their city is a great place to live and work and have fun together.

Where do you live? No matter where you live, you live in a **community**. A community is a place where people live, work, play, and help each other. All communities have homes. They have places for people to work and places to have fun, too.

Is your community near a river? Is the land hilly, or is it flat? Are there grasslands or forests nearby? Thinking about **geography** helps us understand communities. Geography is the study of Earth and the way people and animals live on it.

Let's look at Raleigh, a community in North Carolina. Raleigh was built close to a major road. People who traveled on the road stopped in Raleigh to eat and rest. Being close to this road helped Raleigh grow. Soon it became an important city.

▲ Some people in Raleigh work at this farmers' market.

QUICK CHECK

Main Idea and Details **What is a community?**

5

B WORK AND PLAY

What do people in your community do for work? For fun? The people of Raleigh work at many kinds of jobs. They have different ways to have fun, too.

Work in Raleigh

Raleigh is the **capital** of the state of North Carolina. A capital is a city where a country or state has its government. Some people in Raleigh work for the state government.

Other people in Raleigh work as doctors, teachers, or construction workers. A community like Raleigh needs people with many different skills. People in Raleigh use these different skills to help each other.

▲ Some people in Raleigh construct houses.

Fun in Raleigh

In Raleigh there are many ways to have fun outdoors. You can fish at Shelley Lake, hike in Umstead State Park, or canoe along the Neuse River Canoe Trail. There is an arts **festival** every spring, too. A festival is a celebration. You can listen to music and see artists show their paintings.

The Neuse River Festival is held once a year. At this festival, you can enjoy a free concert, boat races, and picnics. Many people work together to make these festivals successful.

▼ People in Raleigh can canoe on the Neuse River.

QUICK CHECK

Summarize **What are some kinds of work people do in Raleigh?**

▼ The North Carolina State Fair is held in Raleigh.

Volunteers pick up extra food.

Trucks bring the food to centers where it is packed in boxes.

C HELPING HANDS

Communities are places where people help each other. Jill Staton Bullard and her friend Maxine Solomon wanted to help people in Raleigh who didn't have enough to eat. So they started a food sharing program.

Program Helpers at Work

At first Bullard used her car to pick up unsold food from restaurants or stores. Today the program uses 12 trucks to pick up 5 million pounds of food each year.

Helpers do many things. Some pack groceries in boxes to get the food ready for pickup. Others deliver meals.

The program also teaches men and women how to cook. The new cooks make meals for people who cannot cook for themselves.

PEOPLE

One day **Jill Staton Bullard** saw food being thrown away at a fast food restaurant. Bullard started a food sharing program so less food would be wasted. Bullard has won many awards for her service to the people of Raleigh.

Jill Staton Bullard

Other volunteers cook meals for people who need food.

Now more people in the community have enough to eat.

Now more people have food to eat, and the food doesn't get wasted. The workers feel good about helping others, too. Bullard said,

" I am so grateful to be involved with these dedicated people. **"**

QUICK CHECK

Summarize **How do people in the food sharing program help the community?**

Check Understanding

1. **VOCABULARY** Write one sentence for each vocabulary word below.
   community   geography   festival

2. **READING SKILL Main Idea and Details** Use your chart from page 4 to write a paragraph about ways people live, work, and play in Raleigh.

Main Idea	Details

3. **Write About It** Make a list of some ways to have fun in your community.

9

Map and Globe Skills

Use Intermediate Directions

VOCABULARY

cardinal direction

intermediate direction

You know that the compass rose on a map shows north, east, south, and west. These are the **cardinal directions**. A compass rose can also show **intermediate directions**. An intermediate direction is halfway between two cardinal directions.

Learn It

Follow these steps for using a compass rose to find the cardinal and intermediate directions.

- The long points of the compass rose show the cardinal directions. The letters **N**, **E**, **S**, and **W** stand for north, east, south, and west.

- The short points of the compass rose show the intermediate directions. For example, northeast is halfway between north and east. The abbreviations **NE**, **SE**, **SW**, and **NW** stand for northeast, southeast, southwest, and northwest. Intermediate directions are not always labeled on a compass rose.

Try It

Study the compass rose. Use it to answer the questions.

● Which intermediate direction is halfway between north and east?

● What two cardinal directions is southwest between?

Apply It

The map below shows the states near the Great Lakes. Use the map to answer the questions.

● If you go from Duluth to Buffalo, in what direction are you going?

● What direction would you go to travel from Chicago to Bay City?

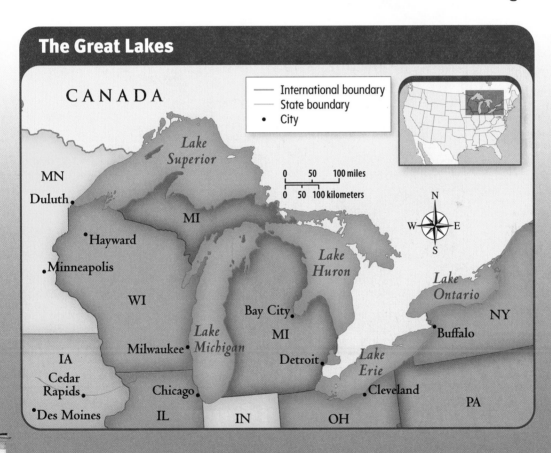

The Great Lakes

CANADA

	International boundary
	State boundary
●	City

Lake Superior

MN
Duluth

MI

Hayward

Minneapolis

0 50 100 miles
0 50 100 kilometers

N
W · E
S

Lake Huron

Lake Ontario

WI

Bay City

NY

Lake Michigan

MI

Buffalo

IA
Cedar Rapids

Milwaukee

Detroit

Lake Erie

Des Moines

Chicago

Cleveland

PA

IL

IN

OH

Communities Big and Small

VOCABULARY

urban p. 13

suburb p. 14

rural p. 15

commute p. 16

transportation p. 16

READING SKILL

Main Idea and Details
Copy the chart below.
As you read fill it with a
main idea and details that
describe a suburb.

Main Idea	Details

STANDARDS FOCUS

SOCIAL STUDIES People, Places, and Environments

GEOGRAPHY Places and Regions

Cleveland, Ohio

Visual Preview

How are communities different?

A City communities are filled with many people and tall buildings.

B Areas that are just outside of cities have more space and fewer people.

C In other communities people may live far from one another.

12

A LOOK AT CITIES

A

New York City has about 8 million people. That's a big city! Only 15 people live in Dellview, North Carolina. That's a very small community.

Cleveland, Ohio, is a big city, with almost half a million people. It is an **urban** area—a city and the communities that surround it. Urban areas like Cleveland have many tall buildings close together.

There's lots to see and do in urban areas. In Cleveland you can visit the Rock and Roll Hall of Fame and Museum, or go to a ball game. On hot summer days you can go to the beach on Lake Erie, one of the five Great Lakes.

Like other cities, Cleveland is made up of neighborhoods. People from Eastern Europe moved to one neighborhood known as Slavic Village. You can still hear Slavic languages, such as Polish and Czech, there. You can taste Slavic foods and listen to Slavic music, too.

▲ People enjoy watching baseball games at Jacobs Field in Cleveland.

QUICK CHECK

Main Idea and Details What makes Cleveland an urban area?

Many cities in the United States have **suburbs** near them. A suburb is a community near a city that has its own homes and stores, and its own schools. Houses and stores in a suburban area are farther apart than in a city. Sidewalks and streets are less crowded, too. Most people drive cars to get around. They might drive to a mall to shop.

URBAN Children playing in city parks usually see tall buildings around them.

Urban

SUBURBAN Homes are farther apart in a suburban area. You might walk or take a bus to school.

Suburban

Farms and Open Land

If you live on a farm or a ranch, or in a small town or village near farms and ranches, you live in a **rural** community. A rural community is one that has farms and open land around it. Rural communities have fewer people than suburbs.

About 300 people live in the rural community of Agra, Kansas. Agra has many farms and ranches—some are bigger than the town itself! If you lived there, your best friend might live on a farm ten miles away.

QUICK CHECK

Summarize **How are suburbs and rural communities different?**

RURAL In a rural area there's enough room to keep a pet like this mule.

Rural

Chicago, Illinois, is a big city. There are a lot of jobs there, but many of the people who work in Chicago do not live there. Instead they live in suburbs like Oak Park and **commute** to their jobs in Chicago. To commute means to travel a distance to and from work.

Some commuters drive their cars to work in Chicago, but the roads get pretty crowded. So many commuters use other kinds of **transportation**. Transportation means a way to get from one place to another. Some use public transportation, such as a bus or train. The fastest way to commute from Oak Park to Chicago is by train— it only takes about twenty minutes.

How many kinds of transportation can you find in this photo of Chicago? ▼

Homes in rural communities are far apart.

Traveling Takes Time

People who live in rural areas often have to drive to another community to get what they need. If you lived in Agra, Kansas, you would go to school in Kirwin, about six miles away. Agra does not have its own school. Agra has some stores, but for some things you need you might go to Phillipsburg, about fifteen minutes away. To visit Topeka, the capital of Kansas, you would have to travel more than four hours!

QUICK CHECK

Main Idea and Details **How do people in Oak Park commute to and from Chicago?**

Check Understanding

1. **VOCABULARY** Use the words below to write a description of an urban community.

   urban   suburb   commute

2. **READING SKILL Main Idea and Details** Use your chart from page 12 to write a paragraph about suburbs.

Main Idea	Details

EXPLORE The Big Idea

3. **Write About It** Write a letter to a friend explaining where you would choose to live and why.

Lesson 3

VOCABULARY

landform p. 19

adapt p. 19

region p. 20

plain p. 20

plateau p. 21

natural resource p. 23

READING SKILL

Main Idea and Details

Copy the chart below. As you read list how landforms and weather affect daily life.

Main Idea	Details

STANDARDS FOCUS

SOCIAL STUDIES People, Places, and Environments

GEOGRAPHY Physical Systems

Our Country's Geography

A view of the Grand Canyon in Arizona

How does geography affect people in a community?

Visual Preview

A Geography affects the homes people build.

B Different types of land affect how people live, travel, and work.

C Water covers much of Earth and people use it in many ways.

D People adapt to weather and climate wherever they live.

A LAND AND PEOPLE

If you could fly like a bird across the United States, you'd see snow-covered mountains, sandy deserts, dark forests, and rushing waters. So many kinds of land and water!

Our country has mountains, hills, valleys, and flat land. These are **landforms**, or shapes of Earth's surface. Landforms are part of geography, and they affect how people live. Water is part of geography, too. People **adapt** to the landforms and water in their communities. To adapt means to change the way you live.

The photo below shows Creek Street in Ketchikan, Alaska. The creek is near the sea, so the water level in the creek rises with the tide in the sea. People who live on Creek Street built their houses on stilts, or posts, to keep the homes above the water. This is how they adapt to the geography of their area.

People affect geography, too. They change the land when they build roads, tunnels, bridges, and buildings.

QUICK CHECK

Main Idea and Details **How did people in Ketchikan adapt to the geography?**

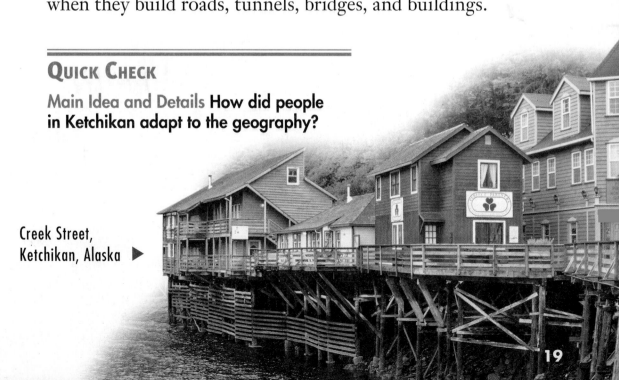

Creek Street,
Ketchikan, Alaska ▶

B TYPES OF LAND

The United States is a really big country with many kinds of land. To make learning about it easier, we can think of the country as having five **regions**—the Northeast, Southeast, Midwest, Southwest, and West. A region is an area with things in common—like geography. The landforms in each region make the region different from other areas. Look at the map to see the different landforms in each region.

Landforms Affect Daily Life

Pete lives on a mountain in the West. In the winter when it snows, traveling up and down the mountain is hard. Pete's dad needs special tires on his car to make it easier to drive in ice and snow. So the mountain affects how Pete's family lives. Landforms in other regions affect how people live, too.

Our country's tallest mountains are in the West, but other regions have mountains, too.

West

Much of the Midwest is flat land as far as the eye can see. This flat land, called a **plain**, is good for farming.

QUICK CHECK

Summarize Which region has land that is flat with no mountains?

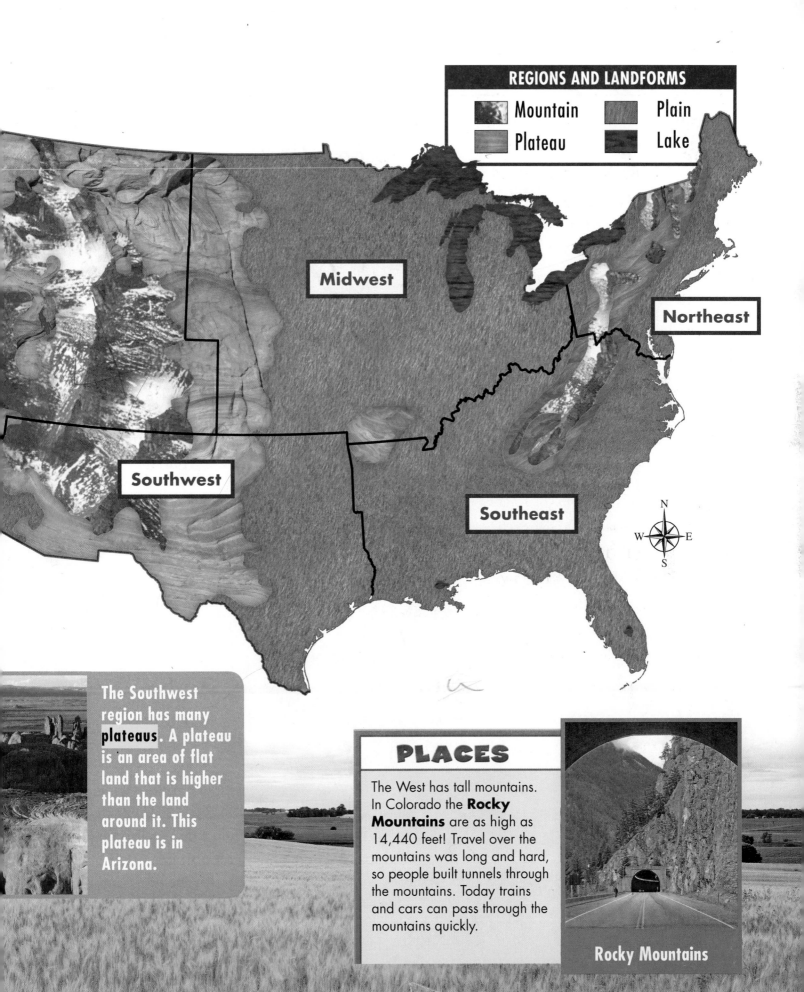

REGIONS AND LANDFORMS

- Mountain
- Plateau
- Plain
- Lake

Midwest

Northeast

Southwest

Southeast

N
W E
S

The Southwest region has many **plateaus**. A plateau is an area of flat land that is higher than the land around it. This plateau is in Arizona.

PLACES

The West has tall mountains. In Colorado the **Rocky Mountains** are as high as 14,440 feet! Travel over the mountains was long and hard, so people built tunnels through the mountains. Today trains and cars can pass through the mountains quickly.

Rocky Mountains

C WATER ALL AROUND US

Did you know that oceans cover most of Earth's surface? Besides lots of ocean, Earth also has lakes, rivers, and ponds. The photo below was taken from outer space and you can see lots of that blue water! Read below to find out more about what Earth looks like from outer space.

Primary Sources

" . . . there emerges [appears] a sparkling blue and white jewel, a . . . sky-blue sphere [round ball] with slowly swirling veils of white, rising gradually like a small pearl in the thick sea of black . . . "

Edgar Mitchell, United States astronaut, January 1971

Write About It What does astronaut Edgar Mitchell compare Earth to?

Using Water

Water is one of our most important **natural resources**. A natural resource is something found in nature that people use. People use water from lakes, rivers, and ponds, for drinking and to grow crops. Most Americans use about 153 gallons every day. How much do you use?

People also use rivers and lakes for transportation. Large boats pull or push barges up and down rivers to move things from place to place. Rivers and lakes are useful for transportation, so many cities are located near rivers.

▲ Water helps these corn stalks grow.

QUICK CHECK

Summarize **What are some things water is used for?**

▼ Riverboats and barges on the Mississippi River

23

ⓓ EFFECTS OF WEATHER

It rained all morning and now there are puddles on the ground. Before you go outside, you put on a rain slicker and rubber rain boots. Then you grab your umbrella. Why? To stay dry! Weather is a part of geography that changes every day.

Climate is the weather in a place or region over a long period of time. Climate tells what the weather is usually like in an area. How does climate affect you? If you live in a cold climate you need warm clothes. You may live in a different kind of house than people who live where it is always warm.

Blizzards are heavy snowstorms with very strong winds. ▼

▲ Tornadoes have strong winds that form a funnel-shaped cloud.

▲ Hurricanes are storms with very strong winds and heavy rain.

Dangerous Weather

Some weather—like tornadoes, hurricanes, and blizzards—can be dangerous. People who live in communities that may have dangerous weather adapt to keep safe. For example, many people in Florida now build strong homes that hurricane winds cannot easily destroy or damage.

QUICK CHECK

Main Idea and Details **How do people adapt to the climate where they live?**

Check Understanding

1. **VOCABULARY** Write one sentence for each vocabulary term below.
   landform   **region**   **natural resource**

2. **READING SKILL** Main Idea and Details Use your chart from page 18 to write how weather and landforms affect daily life.

Main Idea	Details

3. **Write About It** Write a paragraph telling one way people have changed water or a landform in your area.

Map and Globe Skills

Use a Map Scale

VOCABULARY

map scale

A map is always much smaller than the place it shows. So a map uses a **map scale** to show the real distances between two places on a map.

Learn It

- Read the title of the map on page 27. This map shows part of Chicago, Illinois.

- Look at the map scale. The line is two inches long. The map scale shows that 2 inches on the map equals 1 mile on Earth.

- Place the edge of a piece of paper under Union Station and Millennium Park. Make two marks on the paper—one at the dot for Union Station and the other at the dot for Millennium Park. Now put your paper on the map scale and place your first mark under the zero. Where is your second mark? The distance from Union Station to Millennium Park is almost 1 mile.

Try It

Using your map scale, measure distances on the map.

- Is the distance from City Hall to the Art Institute of Chicago more or less than 1 mile?

- Is it more or less than 1 mile from City Hall to Soldier Field?

Apply It

- About how far is it from Northerly Island to Northwestern University?

- About how far is it from the Civic Opera House to Buckingham Fountain?

- How would you use the scale to measure 2 miles on the map?

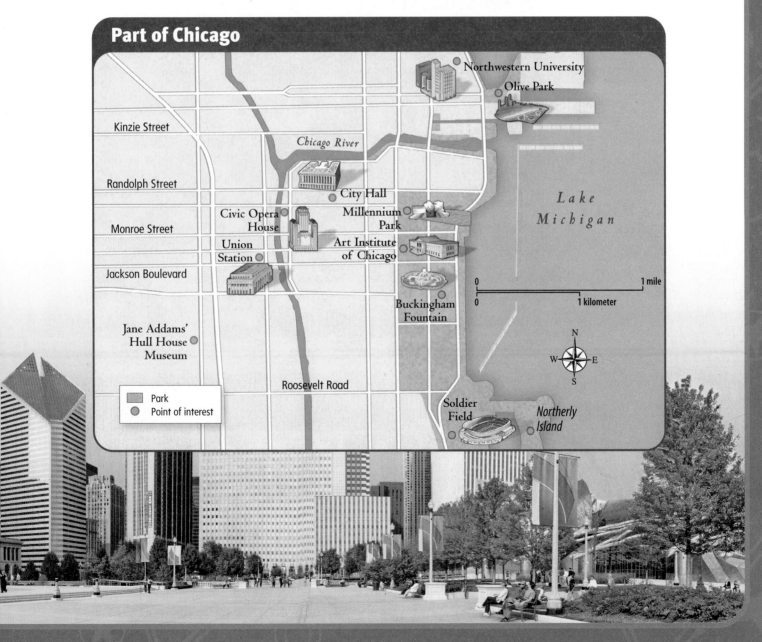

Part of Chicago

Northwestern University
Olive Park
Kinzie Street
Chicago River
Randolph Street
City Hall
Civic Opera House
Millennium Park
Monroe Street
Union Station
Art Institute of Chicago
Lake Michigan
Jackson Boulevard
Buckingham Fountain
0   1 mile
0   1 kilometer
Jane Addams' Hull House Museum
N
W   E
S
Roosevelt Road
Park
Point of interest
Soldier Field
Northerly Island

OUR NATURAL RESOURCES

VOCABULARY

mineral p. 29

nonrenewable resource p. 30

environment p. 32

recycle p. 34

READING SKILL

Main Idea and Details
Copy the chart below. As you read, list how you can protect natural resources.

Main Idea	Details

STANDARDS FOCUS

SOCIAL STUDIES Production, Distribution, and Consumption

GEOGRAPHY Environment and Society

Trees are an important natural resource.

Visual Preview

How do we get and use our natural resources?

A Minerals like copper and salt are found in the ground.

B Oil is a very important resource that cannot be replaced.

C We must protect our resources and use them wisely.

D People can work together to save natural resources.

USING NATURAL RESOURCES

Every day you use pencils and paper in school. You get water from the faucet to drink. You add salt to your food at dinner. Where do these things come from?

What do air, water, soil, plants, and animals have in common? They are all natural resources. We use natural resources every day. We breathe air and drink water. We grow crops using soil, and make paper and other things from the wood of trees.

Can you name something that comes from the ground that you sprinkle on your food? It's salt, of course! Salt is a **mineral**. Minerals are natural resources—they are found in nature, but they are not plants or animals. Salt, coal, and copper are minerals. Coal is burned as fuel, and copper is used in many things, including wire and coins.

QUICK CHECK

Main Idea and Details **What are some ways people use natural resources?**

Copper is dug from the huge Kennecott Copper Mine in Utah.

Nature has many things we need to live. Depending on where they are located, communities have different resources they can use. Communities must also find ways to get resources that may not be found in their area, such as oil or water.

Types of Resources

When you are out of fruit at home, you can buy or pick more fruit. This is an example of replacing something. Water is a renewable resource, a natural resource that can be replaced, or renewed. When it rains or snows, water is replaced in nature. Sunlight, wind, and trees are renewable resources, too.

Other natural resources cannot be replaced. These are **nonrenewable resources**. Oil, copper, coal, iron, and gold are all nonrenewable resources. Oil is a very valuable resource that is used to make gasoline and to heat homes. The United States does not produce all the oil it needs, so we must buy oil from other countries.

Oil rigs in the Gulf of Mexico drill below the ocean floor for oil. ▶

As you can see on the datagraphic, our country's natural resources are found in different regions.

Copper and zinc are used to make pennies. ▼

QUICK CHECK

Summarize **How are renewable resources and nonrenewable resources different?**

DataGraphic
Natural Resources of the United States

Study the map and chart. Then answer the questions.

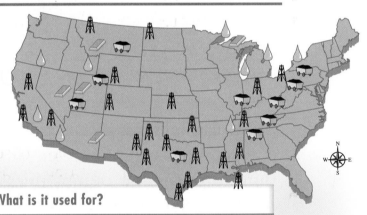

Natural resource	Type of resource	What is it used for?
copper	nonrenewable	jewelry, coins, light bulbs, computer parts, electrical wiring
water	renewable	drinking, washing, cooking, farming, transportation, recreation
oil	nonrenewable	electricity, heat, gasoline, plastics, makeup, lotion, candles, ink, rubber, tires, CDs, DVDs
coal	nonrenewable	electricity, heat, batteries, charcoal, perfume, medicine, rubber cement

Think About Natural Resources

1. Which natural resource on the map is renewable?

2. Which resource is used in plastics, candles, and ink?

▼ Planting new trees
helps to protect
the environment.

© PROTECTING OUR RESOURCES

Our natural resources come from the **environment**—the air, water, land, and other things around us. If communities don't protect their environment, there may not be enough natural resources. People, plants, and animals need clean air to breathe and clean water to drink.

Saving Oil

Oil is a nonrenewable resource that is made into gasoline to run cars. To save oil some companies are making cars that use less gasoline. Other companies make cars that run on fuels that aren't made from oil.

Cars called hybrids run on both gasoline and electricity, so they use less oil. ▶

How Can People Help?

People need to protect the environment. One way is by building "green buildings." A green building has features that make it environmentally friendly. The Hearst Tower in New York City is a green building. It has special windows that allow sunshine in, but keep the sun from heating the building too much in the summer. This means it uses less electricity for lights and air conditioners. Rain water is collected on the roof and stored in a tank. Some of the water is used to water plants inside and outside the building. The water is also used for a giant waterfall inside the building.

QUICK CHECK

Summarize **Why do communities need to protect the environment?**

Hearst Tower in New York City ▶

33

D OTHER WAYS TO HELP

You can help the environment by **recycling**, too. To recycle means to reuse something. Glass jars, cans, newspapers, and some plastics can be recycled. They can be made into something that can be used again. Recyling also means that there is less waste to get rid of.

People can work together to help the environment. Earth Force is an environmental group. Students in this group start recycling programs, clean up parks, and teach others about helping our environment.

QUICK CHECK

Main Idea and Details **What can people do to take care of natural resources?**

Caring for Earth is everyone's job. ▼

Check Understanding

1. **VOCABULARY** Use the words below to write a paragraph on natural resources.
   environment   **recycle**

2. **READING SKILL** Main Idea and Details Use your chart from page 28 to write a paragraph about protecting natural resources.

Main Idea	Details

3. **Write About It** Write a paragraph telling one way natural resources affect communities.

Citizenship

Points of View

Should Trees Be Protected?

Most communities have some trees. As communities grow, trees are sometimes cut down to make room for roads or new buildings. Read three points of view on whether special rules are needed to protect trees.

"I'm for saving trees as much as possible. People should not be allowed to cut trees down unless the trees are on their own land and there are plenty of other trees nearby."

Simone
Parkville, Maryland
From an interview, 2006

"Trees can't be everywhere. There has to be room for houses, schools, hospitals, and streets, but if you cut down trees in one place, you should plant them in another place."

Margarita
Glenwood, Arkansas
From an interview, 2006

"People have the right to decide what to do with the trees on their own property but maybe there should be some rules. Maybe people should only be allowed to cut down one-third or one-half of all the trees on their land."

Ryan
Bromall, Pennsylvania
From an interview, 2006

Write About It Explain why the trees in your community should or should not be protected.

People and the Environment

Lesson 5

VOCABULARY

dam p. 37

reservoir p. 37

levee p. 39

ecosystem p. 40

READING SKILL

Main Idea and Details
Copy the chart below. As you read list the main idea and details of the lesson.

Main Idea	Details

STANDARDS FOCUS

| SOCIAL STUDIES | Science, Technology, and Society |
| GEOGRAPHY | Physical Systems |

Hoover Dam holds back the Colorado River and makes electricity for many communities.

Visual Preview

How do people interact with the environment?

A Building dams is one change people may make to the environment.

B People find new ways to get energy that don't harm the environment.

C People work to protect animals and plants and the places they live.

D Some people work to protect special environments.

CHANGING THE ENVIRONMENT

You are sitting on the shore of Lake Mead, the largest man-made lake in the country. It's hard to believe this huge lake wasn't always here.

You've already learned that people adapt to the environment. But they also change the environment to meet their needs. In the 1920s communities and farms in Arizona and Nevada needed more water. The government built Hoover Dam across the Colorado River. A **dam** is a wall across a river or stream that holds back and controls the water.

After the Hoover Dam was built, the water backed up and formed Lake Mead. People use Lake Mead as a **reservoir**, a place to store water. Farmers use this water for crops. The water is also carried through pipes to cities miles away. The dam has another use, too. Water that passes through the dam turns huge machines to make electricity. The electricity is used by communities many miles away.

QUICK CHECK

Main Idea and Details Why are dams sometimes built?

Besides using Lake Mead as a reservoir, people can use it for fun! ▶

◀ Many Earth Day celebrations include parades like this one in Los Angeles, California.

B # HELPING THE ENVIRONMENT

Unfortunately some things people do can hurt the environment. So in some communities people are working to teach people how to protect the environment.

Gaylord Nelson was a United States Senator from Wisconsin. He always cared about protecting the environment. In 1970 Nelson organized the first Earth Day celebration. Nelson wanted a day that would teach people how important it is to take care of our Earth.

Since then many people celebrate Earth Day every year on April 22. People take part in many ways. The Earth Day Groceries Project began in Seattle, Washington, in 1994. Students decorated brown paper grocery bags with messages about the environment. On Earth Day supermarket customers learned about protecting the environment by reading their grocery bags!

Levee

River

◀ This levee along the Mississippi protects homes from floods.

Using Land

St. Louis, Missouri, is built next to the Mississippi River. A **levee** along the river protects St. Louis. A levee is a long wall made of dirt or concrete built next to a river to prevent flooding. Levees protect the cities and farms near the water.

Some people live in windy areas. The wind can be used to turn windmills that make electricity. Wind is a renewable resource. It is also clean and free! Some people build wind farms and use their land to create energy.

EVENT

In 2005 **Hurricane Katrina** hit states in the South. During this powerful storm, the levees protecting New Orleans broke and the city flooded. Many people lost their homes, and some even lost their lives.

Hurricane Katrina, August 2005

QUICK CHECK

Main Idea and Details **Why is Earth Day celebrated?**

A wind farm makes electricity. ▶

39

Plants and animals depend on the environment for things they need to live. Plants use air, water, and sunlight to grow. Animals eat plants or other animals. Animals and plants together are part of an **ecosystem**—a community of living and nonliving things. Many plants and animals can only live in a certain place. If an ecosystem is harmed or changed, all the plants and animals in the ecosystem are affected. If the ecosystem is destroyed, a plant or animal may die out.

In Missouri a group of scientists is studying the prairie ecosystem. A prairie is flat land covered with grasses and flowers. The group works to protect plants like the Missouri bladderpod and animals like the jackrabbit. They want to keep these endangered plants and animals from dying out forever.

Animals and plants need help in other places, too. On the next page, read how people on islands near Africa work to protect animals there.

▲ The eastern puma used to be seen all across the United States. Now it is seen only in the West.

QUICK CHECK

Summarize **Why is it important to protect ecosystems?**

Yellow bladderpods ▼

PLACES

In some places people have drained wetlands to build on the land. But at **Eagle Bluffs**, near Columbia, Missouri, people restored a wetland. The wetland provides homes for special plants and animals.

Eagle Bluffs

Global Connections

Saving Animals

Mauritius, a group of islands near Africa, once had many animals found nowhere else. Two of these were the pink pigeon and the giant tortoise. Then things changed.

▲ The Aldabran Giant Tortoise is similar to the one once found on Mauritius.

Long ago ships brought both rats and cats to Mauritius. Both escaped and began to live on the islands. They ate the birds and the tortoise eggs. People changed the ecosystem, too. They cut the trees where the pigeons nested, and they ate the tortoises. Soon all the tortoises were gone, and there were very few pink pigeons left.

▼ Pink pigeon

Today the people of Mauritius are working to save the pink pigeons. They have made a park to protect places where pigeons nest. They also are raising another kind of tortoise on a nearby island. Someday they may bring these tortoises to live on Mauritius.

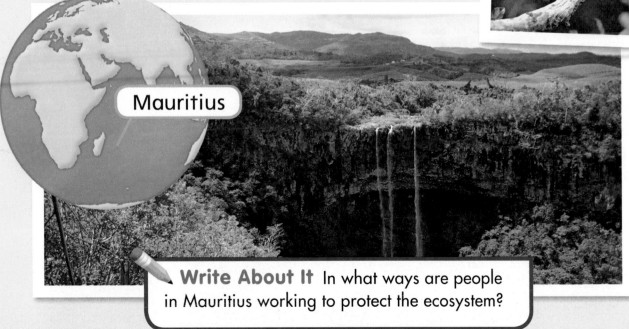

Mauritius

Write About It In what ways are people in Mauritius working to protect the ecosystem?

41

Black tern

Lake sturgeon

Dwarf lake iris

Karner blue butterfly

Lake Superior

Muskellunge

Gray wolf

Lakeside daisy

Lake Michigan

Red-shouldered hawk

Canada lynx

Lake trout

The Great Lakes hold more freshwater than any other place on Earth. The shores of the Great Lakes have prairies, sand dunes, and forests. Hundreds of kinds of fish, turtles, insects, birds, and plants live in and around the lakes.

Around the shores of the lake, though, are cities and factories. People have drained wetlands and cut forests to build homes and businesses. Because of this, almost 30 types of plants and animals now struggle to survive in the Great Lakes. The Hine's emerald dragonfly, for example, lives in wetland and grassy areas. Because people have drained many wetlands, these dragonflies are losing their homes.

A Safe and Healthy Ecosystem

Some people work in groups to keep plants and animals in the Great Lakes safe and healthy. The Great Lakes Basin Ecosystem Team is one such group. They work to protect the ecosystem and to teach visitors how to enjoy the area without harming it.

QUICK CHECK

Main Idea and Details **Why are some animals in the Great Lakes ecosystem endangered?**

▲ Whooping cranes are on the list of birds that need protection.

Yellow perch

Brook trout

Grasshopper sparrow

Eastern prairie fringed orchid

Lake Huron

Lake Erie water snake

Golden-winged warbler

Houghton's goldenrod

Lake Erie

Check Understanding

1. **VOCABULARY** Write one sentence for each of the vocabulary words below.
   dam   reservoir   levee

2. **READING SKILL Main Idea and Details** Use your chart from page 36 to write a paragraph about how people interact with the environment.

Main Idea	Details

EXPLORE The Big Idea

3. **Write About It** Write two or three sentences to explain how dams and levees affect the way people live.

43

Local Connections
Your Community's Land and Resources

Lee lives in Madison, Wisconsin. He learned about the geography and natural resources near his community. Here's what you can do to learn about the geography of your community.

- At the library, find a map of your community that shows landforms. This is also called a topographic map. Look for the landforms and bodies of water near your community, such as mountains, lakes, rivers, oceans, or ponds.

- Use encyclopedias, newspapers, or the Internet to find pictures and information about your community's natural resources.

LOG ON — For more help with your project visit
www.macmillanmh.com

Geography Activity

Make a Clay Landform Model

1 Use a map to learn about the landforms and bodies of water in your area. Decide what to include on your model.

2 Copy the map onto the cardboard. If you decide to make your model larger than the map, you could use a copy machine to make the map larger.

3 Cover the map with clay. Build up each type of feature using different colors of clay.

4 Use your paper to make labels and a key for your model. Use glue, tape, and toothpicks to attach your labels and key to the model.

5 Share your model with your classmates.

Materials
- map of your community
- markers
- cardboard
- clay of different colors
- paper
- glue or tape
- toothpicks

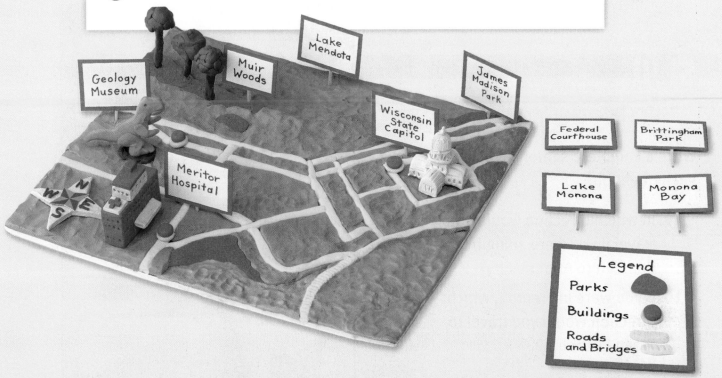

Vocabulary

Number a paper from 1 to 4. Beside each number write the word from below that matches the description.

community   **natural resource**

suburb   **environment**

1. something found in nature that people use
2. a community not far from a city
3. the air, water, land, and living things around us
4. a place where people live, work, play, and help each other

Skill

Use Intermediate Directions

Write a complete sentence to answer each question.

9. In which direction would you travel if you were going from Camden to Atlantic City?
10. If you were in Trenton, which direction would you travel to reach Elizabeth?

Comprehension and Critical Thinking

5. **Reading Skill** Describe three kinds of communities.
6. How can people protect the environment?
7. **Critical Thinking** Why should people in communities help each other?
8. **Critical Thinking** How could a change to the environment be both good and bad?

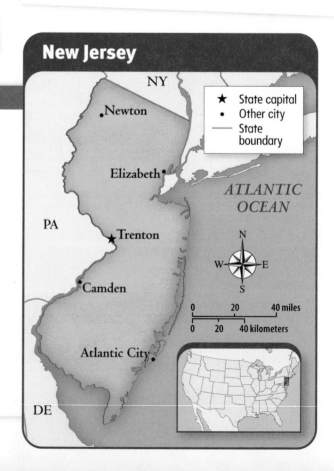

New Jersey

- ★ State capital
- • Other city
- — State boundary

NY

Newton

Elizabeth

PA

Trenton

Camden

ATLANTIC OCEAN

N
W E
S

0   20   40 miles
0   20   40 kilometers

Atlantic City

DE

Test Preparation

Read the paragraphs. Then answer the questions.

The United States has many natural resources. There are tall forests, and areas with rich soil. Lakes and streams provide water. The oceans have fish that people like to eat. Some resources, such as forests, soil, and fish, are renewable.

Renewable resources can be replaced, but people still need to use them wisely. If too many of one kind of fish are taken from the sea, it will take many years for them to be replaced. It is important to use only as much of a renewable resource as we need. That way we will be sure we always have enough.

1. What type of resources are forests, soil, and fish?

A. minerals

B. renewable resources

C. nonrenewable resources

D. animal resources

2. What is the main idea here?

A. Renewable resources can be used again.

B. It is important to use renewable resources wisely.

C. Water is an important resource.

D. There are two types of resources.

3. What are some ways we could protect renewable resources like fish?

4. Oil is an important resource that is used to make oil to heat homes and gasoline to run cars. Name some ways people could use less of this important resource.

5. Name a resource you use every day. Tell whether it is renewable or nonrenewable, and explain how you could use it wisely.

How does where you live affect how you live?

Write About the Big Idea

Expository Essay

Use the Unit 1 foldable to write an essay that answers the Big Idea question, "How does where you live affect how you live?" Begin with an introduction. Write one paragraph for each section of the foldable. Use the notes you wrote on your foldable to help you. End with a paragraph that answers the question.

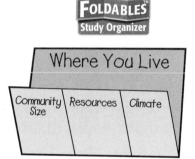

FOLDABLES™
Study Organizer

Where You Live

| Community Size | Resources | Climate |

Projects About the Big Idea

Make a Drawing Think about your community. Draw a picture that shows everyday activities in your community.

Make a Poster Design a poster showing how people use one renewable or one nonrenewable resource. Work in a small group to make a poster that shows the steps needed to bring that resource from nature to your community.

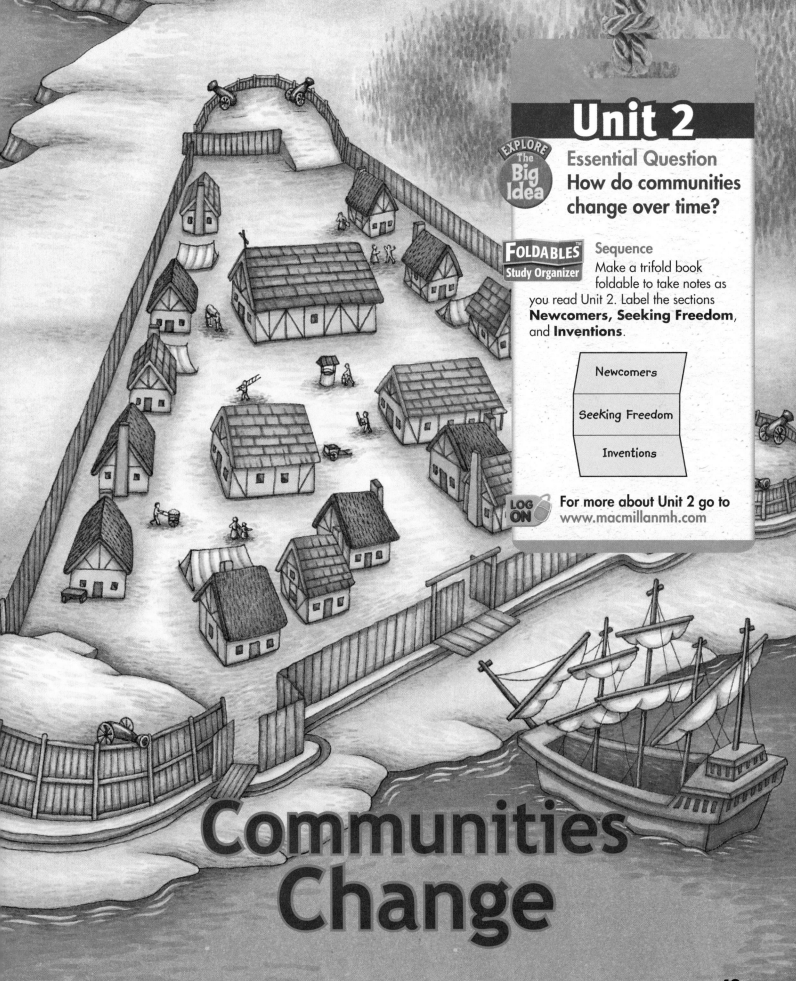

Unit 2

EXPLORE The Big Idea

Essential Question
How do communities change over time?

FOLDABLES™ Study Organizer

Sequence
Make a trifold book foldable to take notes as you read Unit 2. Label the sections **Newcomers, Seeking Freedom**, and **Inventions**.

Newcomers

Seeking Freedom

Inventions

LOG ON For more about Unit 2 go to www.macmillanmh.com

Communities Change

PEOPLE, PLACES, AND EVENTS

Pocahontas

Jamestown

Two Worlds Meet

1607 | People from England first arrive in America.

People from England built a community called **Jamestown**. There they met a good neighbor named **Pocahontas**.

Today you can visit Jamestown and see what life was like back then.

For more about People, Places, and Events, visit www.macmillanmh.com

Colonists

Boston Harbor Today

Boston Tea Party

1773 | Colonists protest British rules by dumping tea into Boston Harbor.

The **colonists** were angry about British rules. They snuck onto British ships and dumped tea into **Boston Harbor**.

Today you can visit the spot where this event, known as the **Boston Tea Party**, took place.

FIRST COMMUNITIES

VOCABULARY

culture p. 53

barter p. 53

artifact p. 53

settler p. 56

slavery p. 59

READING SKILL

Sequence
Copy the chart below. As you read list what happened when new people arrived in America.

First
Next
Last

STANDARDS FOCUS

SOCIAL STUDIES Time, Continuity, and Change

GEOGRAPHY The Uses of Geography

Cahokia was a big Native American city.

Visual Preview

How did the first communities grow?

A Cahokia was built by Native Americans in what is now Illinois.

B The Powhatan, a Native American group, lived in what is now Virginia.

C People from England built a community called Jamestown.

D Africans worked in Jamestown and helped it to grow.

CAHOKIA

It is the year 1200 in the Native American city of Cahokia, in what is now Illinois. From the fields you can see a huge mound of earth, as tall as a ten-story building.

Once the land in this area was nearly flat. Then the people began to build mounds. It took more than 300 years to build the largest mound. At the top the chief and other important people held ceremonies to honor the sun. Sun ceremonies and mound building were all part of the **culture**, or way of life, in Cahokia.

Life in Cahokia

Life in Cahokia was busy. Men fished in nearby rivers. Women and children picked corn and squash to eat. Others made tools and pots to trade in the market.

Cahokia was then one of the biggest cities in the world. It was built near several rivers. People traveled the rivers and **bartered**, or traded goods, with other villages near and far. Trading brought an exchange of things like language, ideas, and technology.

Artifacts, things made or used by people in the past, tell us how people lived long ago.

QUICK CHECK

Sequence **What did Cahokia look like before mound building began?**

Global Connections

Buildings Made Long Ago

About 2,000 years ago, Teotihuacan, Mexico, was at the center of a Native American civilization. A civilization is a culture that has advanced systems of learning, arts, and government. Teotihuacan was even bigger than Cahokia.

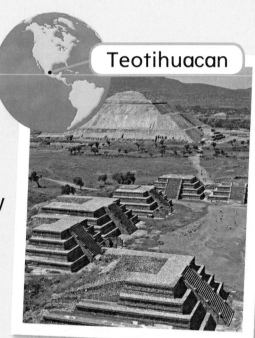
Teotihuacan

People from both Cahokia and Teotihuacan made the mounds and pyramids that we study today. Cahokians built their dirt mounds up to 100 feet tall. Some mounds were used as temples where people worshipped.

The people of Teotihuacan built their huge pyramids of stone. The Pyramid of the Sun is twice the size of the biggest Cahokian mounds! This pyramid has a temple on top.

▲ Some pyramids in Teotihuacan were used to bury the dead.

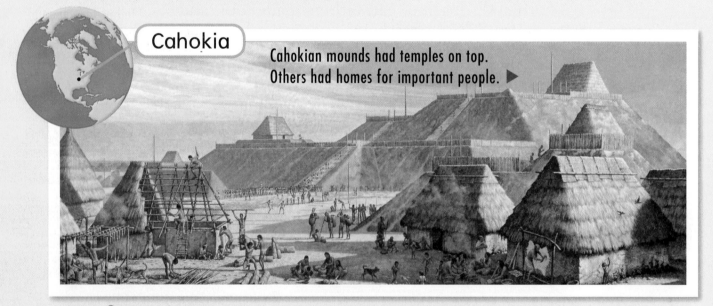
Cahokia

Cahokian mounds had temples on top. Others had homes for important people. ▶

Write About It Write a paragraph about the ways people in Cahokia and Teotihuacan made and used their buildings.

yahikan

canoe

▲ A Powhatan home was called a yahikan. Each had a fire in the center for warmth.

B POWHATAN'S VILLAGES

It is a winter morning in the year 1606. A young girl, Pocahontas, follows her family to the river to bathe. Bathing in the river every day is part of her group's culture. Later she will help her mother make clothing.

Meeting Community Needs

Pocahontas lived in a Native American village in what is now Virginia. Her father, Powhatan, was a powerful chief. During the early 1600s he ruled over many villages. The people he led were also called the Powhatan.

The Powhatan used the natural resources around them to meet many needs. They carved canoes out of trees and used them on the rivers and the ocean to fish and trade. The Powhatan also hunted turkey and deer in the forests. They grew and stored corn and squash. Everyone worked together so there was enough to eat.

▼ The Powhatan used stone knives like these.

QUICK CHECK

Main Idea and Details **How did the Powhatan use resources?**

Do you know why the year 1492 is important? That's when Christopher Columbus discovered America. After that people from many countries in Europe started coming to the Americas. Some came looking for land, gold, or adventure. Others came to build new communities and to find freedom.

Making a New Home

People from England first came to Powhatan lands in 1607. These **settlers** began making this land their home. A settler is a person who moves from one area to another to find land. The settlers called their new home Jamestown. Many of them were unwilling to work. They only wanted to look for gold!

▲ Settlers from England came to America by ship.

Jamestown

Life in Jamestown was very hard in the winter of 1609. The settlers soon ran out of food. One settler wrote, "Now all of us at James Town, beginning to feel that sharp prick of hunger . . . " Even so, new settlers continued to arrive.

You can visit Jamestown Settlement to see how Jamestown looked long ago. ▶

Help From the Powhatan

The land was new and strange to the English. They had to learn how to hunt and grow food. To whom did the settlers go for help? Their neighbors, the Powhatan. Sometimes Pocahontas brought fish, corn, and squash to the hungry settlers. She became friends with Jamestown's leader, John Smith, and later married John Rolfe, another English settler.

As Jamestown grew, there was less land for the Powhatan. In just ten years the Powhatan had lost much of their land to the Jamestown settlers.

QUICK CHECK

Sequence What did the English have to do after settling in Jamestown?

John Smith

Pocahontas

This photo shows how people in Jamestown made glass. ▶

▲ Artifacts help us understand Jamestown. What do you think these glass objects were used for?

Ⓓ HERE TO STAY

Settlers kept coming to Jamestown. As more people arrived, Jamestown grew stronger. Settlers chopped down trees for wood. They planted tobacco. They also made glass. Wood, tobacco, and glass could then be sent back to England for sale.

Growing tobacco was hard work! In 1619 a Dutch ship brought some people from Africa to Jamestown. The English settlers were happy to have the African workers.

Africans in Jamestown

The Africans who came to Jamestown helped it to grow even more. They cooked, made clothes, worked on farms, took care of children, and made buildings.

Though the first Africans in Jamestown did not choose to come and were not free, they were not all kept in **slavery**. Slavery is forcing people to work without pay and without freedom. The first Africans in Jamestown were servants who earned their freedom in time. Slavery would be far worse for the Africans who followed.

QUICK CHECK

Main Idea and Details **What types of work did people do in Jamestown?**

Some Africans who came to Jamestown cooked for the English settlers.

Check Understanding

1. **VOCABULARY** Write one sentence for each vocabulary word below.
   culture   artifact   settler   slavery

2. **READING SKILL** **Sequence** Use the chart from page 52 to write a paragraph about new people arriving in America.

   | First |
   | Next |
   | Last |

3. **EXPLORE The Big Idea** **Write About It** Write a paragraph telling how the English learned to live in their new settlement of Jamestown.

A New Country

VOCABULARY

colony p. 61

tax p. 62

revolution p. 65

Patriot p. 65

constitution p. 66

READING SKILL

Sequence
Copy the chart. As you read fill it in with events that led up to the American Revolution.

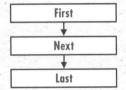

First
Next
Last

STANDARDS FOCUS

SOCIAL STUDIES Time, Continuity, and Change

GEOGRAPHY The Uses of Geography

A mill in Plymouth, Massachusetts

Visual Preview

How did the British colonies grow and become a new country?

A People from Europe built new communities in North America.

B Boston became one of the biggest colonial cities.

C Colonists won their freedom from British rule.

D Leaders wrote a plan for the new government.

A sailor calls, "Land ahead!" You rush to the front of the ship and stare into the mist. Then you see it. America!

After people back in Europe learned about the success of Jamestown, more and more people sailed across the huge Atlantic Ocean. They wanted a chance to start a better life in America, too.

A Better Life

Jamestown wasn't big enough for everyone! Many of the newcomers settled in different areas along the Atlantic coast. By the 1750s there were 13 British **colonies** stretching along the east coast of North America. A colony is a place that is ruled by another country. Most colonists, or people who live in a colony, were farmers who raised crops to sell and make money.

Many British people traveled to America to live in the colonies. Some came for religious freedom. Others came hoping to start a business or to own their own land.

This old map shows the east coast of America in 1770.

▲ Farmers in the colonies grew crops such as corn, rice, and tobacco.

QUICK CHECK

Sequence What happened after people heard about the success of Jamestown?

61

B BOSTON, A COLONIAL CITY

Boston was one of the biggest colonial cities. What was life in Boston like in colonial times? People bought fish from the fishermen and vegetables from their neighbors. They could buy wooden chests, beds, and barrels made right in Boston. But items like silk and tea came from Great Britain.

▲ Colonists bought tea from Great Britain.

Paying Money to the British

Colonists had to pay **taxes** on things from Great Britain. A tax is money paid to a government. A new law called the Stamp Act said that colonists had to pay a tax on items such as sugar, newspapers, tea, paper, and glass. These were things colonists used every day.

People in Boston were unhappy about paying these taxes and started to complain. They were especially angry about the tax on tea. Why should they pay if they didn't have a say in how the tax money was used, they thought.

Unfair Rules

There were other rules the colonists thought were unfair. For example, the colonists were not allowed to meet in groups. They also said they did not get fair trials in courts with judges. Some rules said British soldiers could eat and sleep in colonists' homes whenever they wanted. The colonists knew it was time to make some important changes.

▼ Many things shipped to and from Great Britain passed through Boston's busy harbor.

QUICK CHECK

Main Idea and Details **Why were people in Boston unhappy with the British?**

In 1774 colonial leaders met in the Philadelphia State House, now called Independence Hall. ▶

C TAKING ACTION

Many colonists wanted to let the British government know that they were unhappy with these rules. First they took peaceful actions. Some, like Samuel Adams, wrote newspaper articles. Others met to talk and to make decisions. Many people stopped buying British items such as tea.

These actions weren't enough. Colonists soon took other actions that were not peaceful. In 1773 a group of men, dressed as Native Americans so the British would not recognize them, secretly went onto British ships. As a protest they dumped 342 chests of British tea into Boston Harbor. This event became known as the Boston Tea Party.

▼ As punishment after the Boston Tea Party, Great Britain closed Boston Harbor. No ships could enter or leave.

Fighting for Freedom

The British government would not change its unfair rules. Nothing the colonists did worked. It was time to declare independence in writing. The job of writing such a declaration was given to a Virginia lawyer named Thomas Jefferson.

The Declaration of Independence told King George III of Great Britain that Americans would be free. The colonists' leaders approved the declaration on July 4, 1776. The British king was not happy—and the American **Revolution** began. A revolution is a fight that often leads to the end of one government and the beginning of another. British soldiers came to fight the **Patriots**—the people who fought for independence. After seven years of war, the Patriots finally won independence from Great Britain. The 13 colonies were now a new country—the United States of America.

▲ African Americans were among those who fought during the American Revolution.

QUICK CHECK

Sequence **What happened after colonial leaders approved the Declaration of Independence?**

George Washington

PEOPLE

George Washington was a general who led Patriots during the American Revolution. In 1789 Washington was elected President of the United States of America. We honor President Washington by celebrating his birthday on President's Day, the third Monday in February.

▲ Representatives signed the United States Constitution in 1788.

A new country needs a **constitution**, or a written plan of government. In 1787 representatives, or people who speak or act for others, met in Philadelphia to write a constitution. After talking and thinking about different ideas, they reached a compromise. In 1788 the United States Constitution was approved by the 13 states and was now the law.

QUICK CHECK

Sequence What did representatives need to do after the war was over?

Check Understanding

1. **VOCABULARY** Use the words below to write a paragraph about the Patriots' fight for freedom.

   tax   revolution   constitution

2. **READING SKILL Sequence** Use your chart from page 60 to write a paragraph about the events that led to the American Revolution.

   | First |
   | Next |
   | Last |

3. **Write About It** Write a letter about what it might have been like to live during the American Revolution.

Citizenship

Democracy in Action

Cooperation and Compromise

Like people long ago, people today cooperate and compromise. A fifth-grade class in Lutz, Florida, wanted a dog park at Nye Park. At a town meeting the students found out that Nye Park was too small. So the students compromised and asked for a leash-only dog area. Finally the town agreed to create a dog park elsewhere. Read the steps below to learn how to compromise.

How to Work Together

1. **Identify the problem.** Find out what each group or person thinks is the problem.

2. **Express points of view.** Share the reasons why people disagree. Find out what each person wants.

3. **Look for common goals or interests.** Talk about the ideas or goals that all groups share.

4. **Find ways that everyone can gain from compromise.** Look for a way to give each group or person at least part of what they want, so that everyone can agree.

Write About It Write a paragraph about a school activity that requires cooperation.

Chart and Graph Skills

Use Time Lines

VOCABULARY

time line

year

decade

century

You have read about events in America's history. It is not always easy to remember what happened first, next, and last. A **time line** shows the order of events. Learning to use time lines will help you learn about events in the past.

Learn It

Follow these steps and look at the time line below as you read.

- **Look at the dates.** Time lines are divided to show time periods, such as **years**, **decades**, or **centuries**. A year is any period of 12 months. A decade is 10 years, and a century is 100 years.

- **Look at the order of events.** Events are listed in time order from left to right. The earliest event on this time line is "Christopher Columbus lands in the Americas."

- **Use the dates to tell the number of years between events.** Subtract the date of the earlier event from the date of the later event.

First Communities

1560 - Spanish people come to Powhatan lands

1450   1500   1550   1600   1650

1492 - Christopher Columbus lands in the Americas

1607 - English settlers arrive in Jamestown

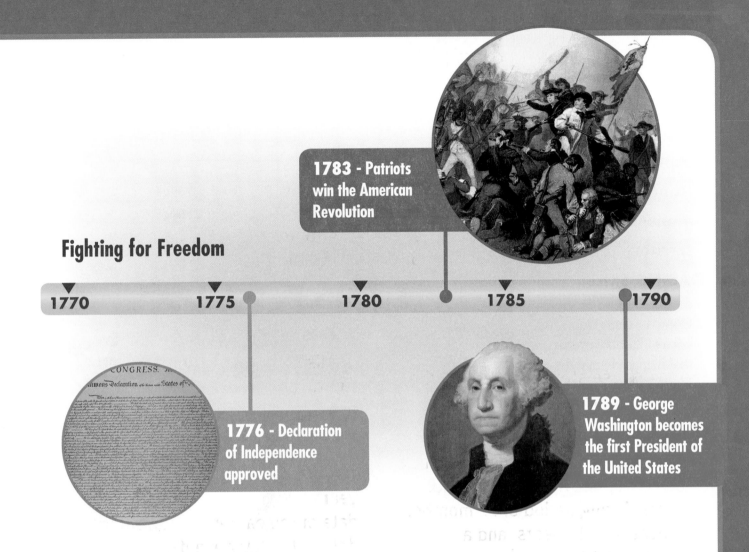

Fighting for Freedom

1783 - Patriots win the American Revolution

1770   1775   1780   1785   1790

1776 - Declaration of Independence approved

1789 - George Washington becomes the first President of the United States

Try It

Use the time line above to answer the questions.

- How many years does this time line cover?

- What is the last event on the time line?

- What happened in 1776?

- How many years after the end of the Revolution did George Washington become President?

Apply It

- Make a time line of your own life.

- Divide your time line into years.

- Make the first event the year you were born.

- Include five important events on your time line. Also include an event in the future—your 13th birthday. In what year will you be 13?

MOVING WEST

Lesson 3

VOCABULARY

explorer p. 71

frontier p. 71

pioneer p. 71

territory p. 72

READING SKILL

Sequence

Copy the chart below. As you read list the events that helped change the United States after the Revolutionary War.

| First |
| Next |
| Last |

STANDARDS FOCUS

SOCIAL STUDIES · Time, Continuity, and Change

GEOGRAPHY · The World in Spatial Terms

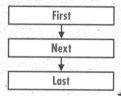

Daniel Boone led people west.

Visual Preview

How did the United States change after the American Revolution?

A As the country grew, people began to move west.

B Lewis and Clark led a team to find out about the land to the west.

C Many people traveled west in covered wagons.

Ⓐ LOOKING WEST

You are traveling west but you are not even on a road.
You are following a Native American
trail over the mountains.

The country was growing quickly! Soon people began thinking about moving west. Daniel Boone was an **explorer** who followed Native American trails west in the 1770s. An explorer is someone who goes to a new place to find out about it. Boone found forests filled with bear, deer, and fox. He also discovered Native American communities as he traveled through the **frontier**. A frontier is the far edge of a country where new people are just beginning to settle.

Boone explored the area that is now Kentucky. Later he helped settlers cross the Appalachian Mountains to make new homes on the other side.

QUICK CHECK

Sequence **What did Daniel Boone do after he explored Kentucky?**

PLACES

Daniel Boone helped build a new settlement in Kentucky called **Fort Boonesborough**. Today people can visit Fort Boonesborough State Park to see what life was like for **pioneers**. A pioneer is the first of a group of people to settle in an area.

Fort Boonesborough

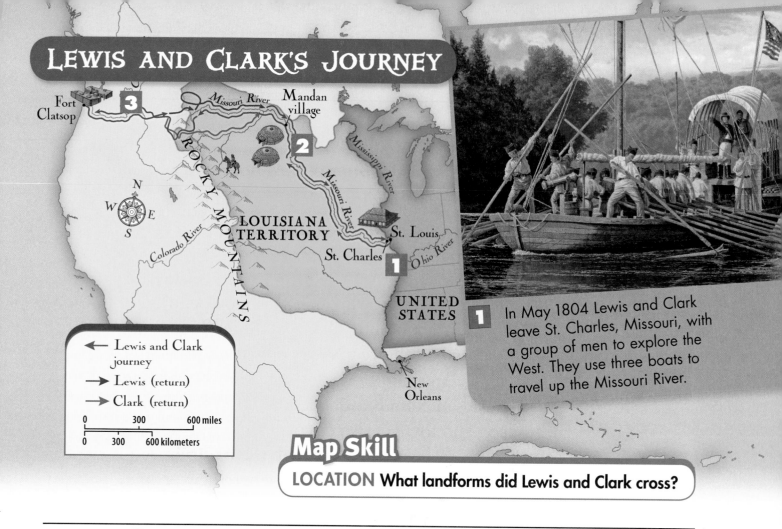

LEWIS AND CLARK'S JOURNEY

Fort Clatsop

3

Missouri River

Mandan village

2

Mississippi River

ROCKY MOUNTAINS

N
W E
S

Colorado River

Missouri River

LOUISIANA TERRITORY

St. Louis

St. Charles

1

Ohio River

UNITED STATES

New Orleans

← Lewis and Clark journey
→ Lewis (return)
→ Clark (return)

0   300   600 miles
0   300   600 kilometers

1 In May 1804 Lewis and Clark leave St. Charles, Missouri, with a group of men to explore the West. They use three boats to travel up the Missouri River.

Map Skill

LOCATION What landforms did Lewis and Clark cross?

B ACROSS THE CONTINENT

The Mississippi River was important for trade and travel. President Thomas Jefferson wanted to get control of the Mississippi River from France. He tried to buy New Orleans, the city where the Mississippi River flows into the sea. Instead, in 1803 France sold all of the Louisiana **Territory**. A territory is land owned by a country. This deal, called the Louisiana Purchase, doubled the size of the United States, all for $15 million!

Learning About the New Land

The United States knew very little about this huge territory. So Jefferson hired Meriwether Lewis and William Clark to go and explore the new land. During their journey Lewis and Clark made maps that would help settlers who moved west later.

2 Lewis and Clark meet a Native American woman named Sacagawea. She travels with them as their guide. She tells them which plants are safe to eat and helps them get horses to finish their journey.

3 Along the way Lewis and Clark study plants and animals and keep careful records of their findings.

People, Plants, and Animals

During their two-year journey, Lewis and Clark met some of the Native Americans who lived in the West. Sacagawea, their Native American guide, helped them talk with the people they met because she knew many of their languages. Lewis and Clark wrote about all these different people and their ways of life.

Lewis and Clark also studied plants and animals. They wrote about at least 170 plants. They also described animals such as the white-tailed deer and the plains gray wolf.

EVENT

The **Louisiana Purchase** included all or part of 15 states and even parts of Canada. In New Orleans the event was celebrated by raising the American flag!

Louisiana Purchase

QUICK CHECK

Summarize What did Lewis and Clark do during their journey?

ⓒ TRAILS TO THE WEST

Pioneers and settlers followed Native American and explorers' trails to the West. Many trails, like the Oregon Trail, began in Independence, Missouri. Settlers often traveled in wagon trains, a group of covered wagons traveling together across country.

The Oregon Trail

The Oregon Trail was difficult to travel. Rivers were good for drinking water, but they were hard to cross. Families always looked for food and fuel for cooking fires. Have you ever written a letter or journal entry about a trip you have taken? Below, read how a 17-year-old girl described her journey on the trail.

Primary Sources

"We traveled but nine miles.... The roads were very hilly and the sand six inches deep. We traded with the Indians this evening for salmon; they are the best fish I ever saw."

Journal Entry
Abigail Jane Scott, August 5, 1852

Write About It Write a paragraph describing what Scott's journal entry tells you about traveling on the Oregon Trail.

Traveling by wagon train was slow and difficult.

Why Move West?

By 1870 thousands of pioneers had traveled across the Oregon Trail. Many had listened to the words of John Soule, an Indiana journalist who said,

> **"** Go West, young man, and grow up with the country. **"**

Some settlers started farms in Oregon. Others hoped to find gold in California! Others went just for adventure. All who went west hoped for better lives.

QUICK CHECK

Main Idea and Details **Why did pioneers travel the Oregon Trail?**

Check Understanding

1. **VOCABULARY** Make a drawing that shows the meaning of each word below.
   explorer   **frontier**   **pioneer**

2. **READING SKILL** Sequence Use your chart from page 70 to write a paragraph telling how the United States changed after the American Revolution.

First
Next
Last

3. **Write About It** Write a diary entry that a pioneer traveling west might have written.

Map and Globe Skills
Understanding Hemispheres

VOCABULARY

sphere

hemisphere

prime meridian

equator

Today people come to the United States from all over the world. You can find these places on a globe, a model of Earth. A globe is a **sphere**. It is round, like a ball. You can see only half of a globe at a time. The part of the globe that you see is called a **hemisphere**, which means "half of a sphere."

Learn It

We can divide Earth two ways— around the middle or top to bottom.

- The **equator** is an imaginary line around Earth halfway between the North Pole and the South Pole. Any place north of this line is in the Northern Hemisphere. Any place south of this line is in the Southern Hemisphere.

- The **prime meridian** is an imaginary line that runs from the North Pole to the South Pole through Greenwich, England. Places east of this line are in the Eastern Hemisphere. Places west of this line are in the Western Hemisphere.

- A continent can lie in more than one hemisphere.

Western Hemisphere

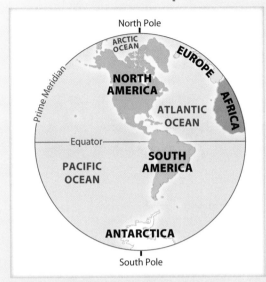

Eastern Hemisphere

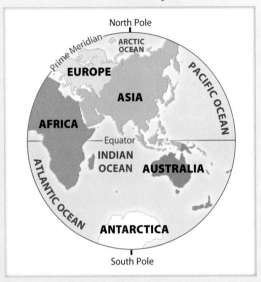

Northern Hemisphere

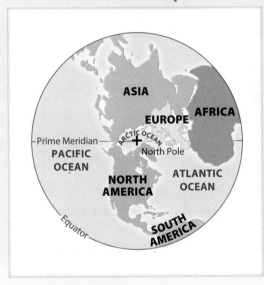

Southern Hemisphere

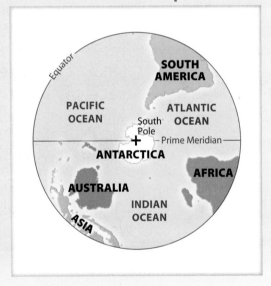

Try It

Look at the maps above.

- Name the four hemispheres.

- Which hemisphere is entirely south of the equator?

Apply It

- Which two hemispheres is North America in?

- Which two hemispheres is Australia in?

COMMUNITIES BECOME CITIES

Lesson 4

VOCABULARY

industry p. 79

immigrant p. 80

migration p. 82

discrimination p. 83

READING SKILL

Sequence

Copy the chart below. As you read list ways small towns and cities grew.

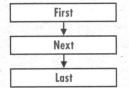

| First |
| Next |
| Last |

STANDARDS FOCUS

SOCIAL STUDIES — Time, Continuity, and Change

GEOGRAPHY — Human Systems

The Statue of Liberty greeted newcomers.

Visual Preview

How did small communities grow into large cities?

A As more people moved to find jobs, small towns grew into cities.

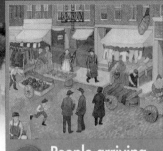

B People arriving from other countries helped cities grow.

C Many African Americans moved to cities in the North and Midwest.

New York City was once a small town with just a few streets and buildings. Today it is our country's largest city, with more than 8 million people!

When the population of a place grows, communities grow, too. Population means the number of people who live in an area. More people means more houses, schools, and roads. Soon towns become small cities. Small cities may grow into large urban areas.

What makes a population grow? One answer is jobs! People often move to new places to find work. For example, many people moved to northern Pennsylvania to get jobs in the coal **industry**. An industry makes one kind of product or provides one kind of service. Coal mining is an industry. So is banking.

Geography also affects population. People often move to a new place because of its geography. Some people like a warm climate. They move to an area where it is warm.

QUICK CHECK

Sequence **What happens after new people move to an area?**

Many women found jobs in clothing factories. ▶

79

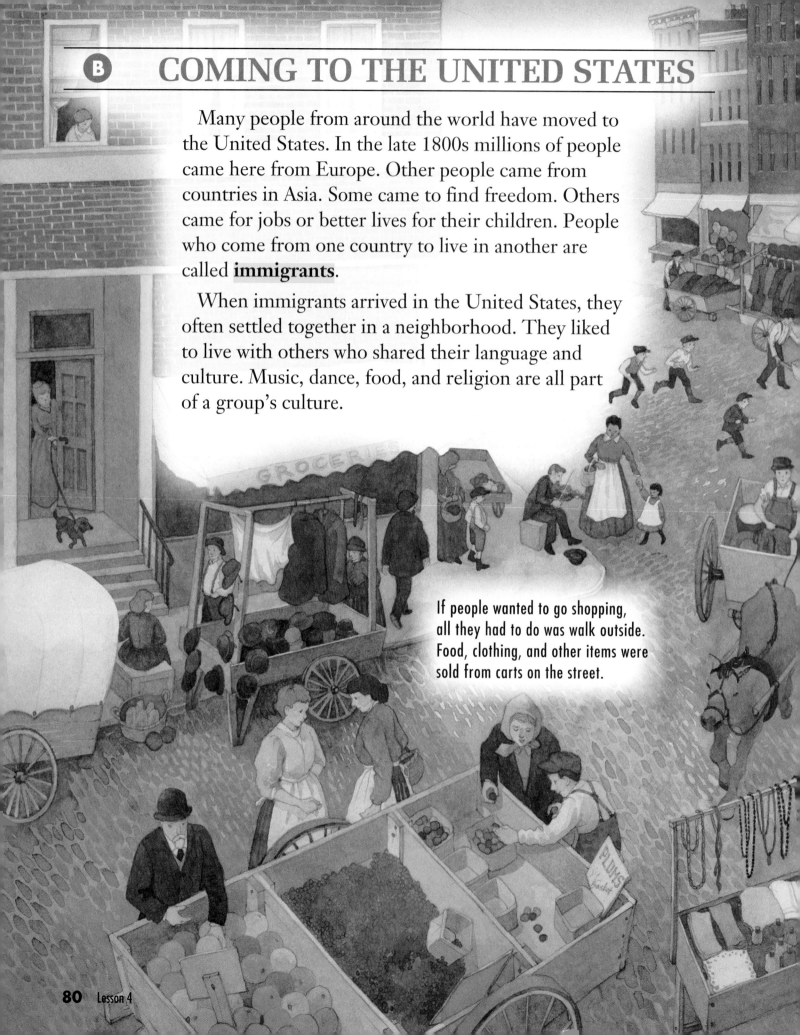

Many people from around the world have moved to the United States. In the late 1800s millions of people came here from Europe. Other people came from countries in Asia. Some came to find freedom. Others came for jobs or better lives for their children. People who come from one country to live in another are called **immigrants**.

When immigrants arrived in the United States, they often settled together in a neighborhood. They liked to live with others who shared their language and culture. Music, dance, food, and religion are all part of a group's culture.

If people wanted to go shopping, all they had to do was walk outside. Food, clothing, and other items were sold from carts on the street.

With large numbers of immigrants, the populations of cities grew. The streets were often filled with traffic. In New York City most immigrants lived in tenements—apartment buildings with many people.

Sometimes musicians, dancers, and other performers provided entertainment for people living in and visiting a neighborhood.

Sometimes immigrants moved into communities that were already settled. Over time, their culture helped shape the neighborhood. For example, some neighborhood restaurants serve food from a particular culture, and museums show paintings made by immigrant artists.

QUICK CHECK

Main Idea and Details **How do immigrants change communities?**

PEOPLE

Many **immigrant** parents came to this country so their children could have a better education. When they weren't in school, many immigrant children worked to help earn money.

Immigrants

About the same time that immigrants were arriving from other countries, people were also on the move in the United States. Many African Americans in the South decided to move to the North and the Midwest. This **migration**, or movement from one part of a country to another, changed our country. Thousands of African Americans left farms in the South and moved to big cities like New York, Chicago, Detroit, and Pittsburgh to find work in factories.

Those that moved had to adapt to life in an urban community. They now lived in crowded cities full of people, tall buildings, and traffic. Life was very different from life on farms in the rural South.

▼ The movement of African Americans from the South to the North became known as the Great Migration.

▲ African Americans at work in New York around 1917

Life in the North

Like the immigrants, African Americans were looking for a better life. In the South they faced **discrimination**. Discrimination happens when people are treated unfairly because of how they look or what they believe. They faced discrimination in the North, too, but life was better for them there. People found jobs and some started their own businesses.

QUICK CHECK

Compare and Contrast **How is migration different from immigration?**

Check Understanding

1. **VOCABULARY** Write one sentence for each vocabulary word below.
immigrant migration discrimination

2. **READING SKILL Sequence**
Use your chart from page 78 to write a paragraph about how small towns grew into cities.

First
Next
Last

3. **Write About It** Write a paragraph that tells how immigrants added to America's way of life.

Chart and Graph Skills

Use Bar Graphs

VOCABULARY

graph

bar graph

You have read about changes in population and the growth of cities. You can learn information about population by reading a **graph**. A graph is a special kind of picture that shows information in a way that is easy to understand. A **bar graph** uses bars to show information. You can use bar graphs to compare amounts of different items.

Learn It

Look at the graph as you follow the steps.

- **Read the title.** The graph shows the population of New York City from 1900 to 1930.

- **Read the labels.** The labels along the bottom show the years the graph is about. The labels along the side show the number of people in millions.

- **Put the information together.** Put your finger at the top of the blue bar, the bar for 1920. Move your finger to the left. You can see the blue bar reaches just past the mark for 5 million. This means that in 1920 the population of New York City was just over 5 million people. In which year shown on the graph did New York City have the lowest population?

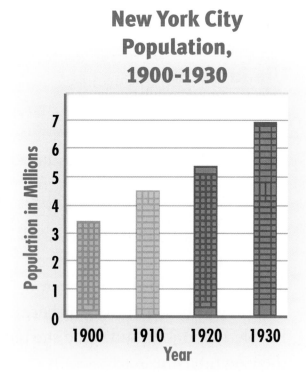

New York City Population, 1900-1930

Try It

Now look at the graph on this page to answer the questions.

- What does this graph show?

- What do the bars stand for?

- About how many people lived in Boston in 1920?

Apply It

Find out the number of students in each class in your school. Show the information on a bar graph. Decide which information will go along the bottom and the side of the graph. Give your graph a title.

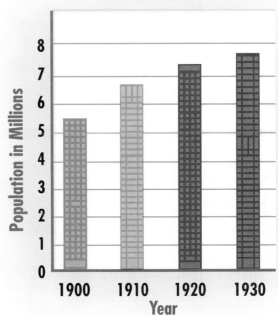

Boston Population, 1900-1930

Population in Millions

8
7
6
5
4
3
2
1
0

1900   1910   1920   1930

Year

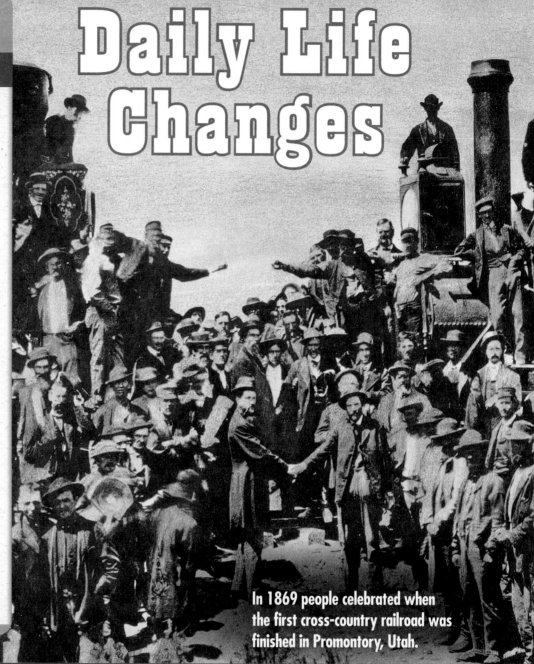

Daily Life Changes

Lesson 5

VOCABULARY

transcontinental p.87

skyscraper p. 89

elevator p. 89

manufacture p. 91

assembly line p. 91

READING SKILL

Sequence
Copy the chart below. As you read list the events that changed daily life in the United States.

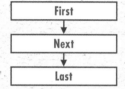

| First |
| Next |
| Last |

STANDARDS FOCUS

SOCIAL STUDIES Science, Technology, and Society

GEOGRAPHY Environment and Society

In 1869 people celebrated when the first cross-country railroad was finished in Promontory, Utah.

Visual Preview

How did inventions change lives in the mid-1800s?

A By 1869 railroad lines stretched across the country.

B New inventions improved lives in many ways.

C Automobiles and other inventions improved ways of traveling.

A TRAVELING MADE EASIER

As the eastern part of the United States got even more crowded, people began moving west. Traveling was hard. There were no trains, airplanes, cars, or even roads!

As more people moved west, a safer, faster way to travel was needed. Traveling west by wagon or ship took too long. In 1862 workers began building the first **transcontinental** railroad. This railroad ran across the continent. The Central Pacific Railroad was built eastward from Sacramento, California, mostly by Chinese immigrants. Irish immigrants worked on the Union Pacific Railroad, which was built westward from Omaha, Nebraska.

The two railroads met in Promontory, Utah, in 1869. Now travel that used to take months took only days. Railroads also made it easier to carry things, like food and mail, between the East and the West.

QUICK CHECK

Sequence How many years after work began on the transcontinental railroad was it completed?

▲ The Golden Spike was the last spike used to finish the transcontinental railroad.

NEW WAYS OF DOING THINGS

The railroad was an invention that helped people travel faster than they had before. An invention is something that has been made for the first time. As new communities and industries grew, people made more inventions that changed life everywhere.

Before

◄ **1830** Until the 1830s news traveled only as fast as a galloping horse. It could take days for news to travel across the country.

1853 Climbing many stairs wasn't easy, so most buildings were only a few stories tall.

◄ **1879** If you wanted to see at night you had to light a candle or an oil lamp. This was dangerous—fires could start easily.

1955 Germs spread in crowded cities. Schools and public places were sometimes closed so people couldn't pass on sicknesses.

PEOPLE

After **Granville T. Woods** invented a railway telegraph in 1887, train operators could send and receive messages between moving trains and the station. This helped people keep track of where trains were. It also helped prevent accidents.

Granville T. Woods

Inventions Change Communities

How did inventions change communities? Very tall building called **skyscrapers** made it possible for more people to work and live in big cities. Changes in medicine helped people avoid getting sick. Inventions made life easier and communities safer.

After

Joseph Henry invented the telegraph in 1830, but it was not until 1843 that telegraph lines were put up. Then news could travel with lightning speed.
1830 ▶

In 1853 Elisha Otis made the first safe **elevator**, a machine for moving people up and down in a building. Now buildings could be taller.
1853

After 1879 when Thomas Edison improved the lightbulb, homes, workplaces, and schools got much brighter and a lot safer, too.
1879 ▶

In 1955 Jonas Salk made a vaccine that prevented a serious disease called polio. Vaccines made it safer for people to live in crowded cities.
1955

QUICK CHECK

Sequence **Why do you think skyscrapers weren't built until after the elevator was invented?**

MORE WAYS TO GET AROUND

By the early 1900s people had invented even faster ways to travel—cars and airplanes. People could travel longer distances and make trips faster with these new forms of transportation. The Datagraphic below shows how these better forms of transportation changed the time it took to cross the country.

DataGraphic
Changes in Transportation

Study the map and pictograph below.
Then answer the questions that follow.

From New York City to San Francisco

1860 stagecoach		☀☀☀☀☀☀☀☀☀☀ ☀☀☀☀☀☀☀☀☀☀
1869 train		☀☀☀☀ ☀☀☀ ☀☀
1925 car		☀☀ ☀☀
1935 airplane		☀

☀ = 1 day of travel

Think About Changes in Transportation

1. About how many days did it take to travel by train from New York City to San Francisco in 1869?

2. About how many miles is it from New York to San Francisco?

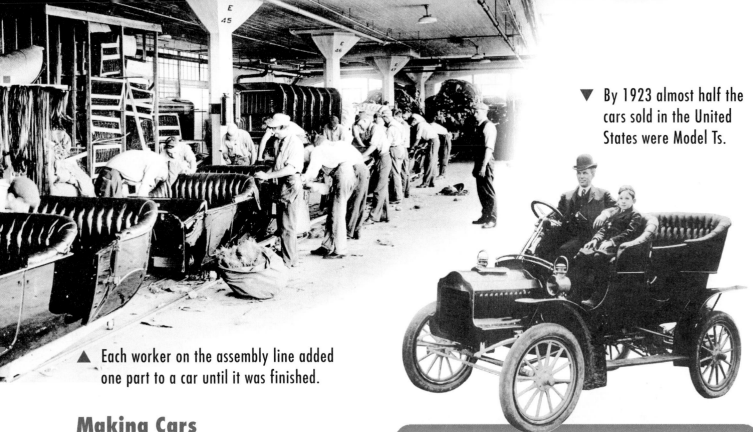

▲ Each worker on the assembly line added one part to a car until it was finished.

▼ By 1923 almost half the cars sold in the United States were Model Ts.

Making Cars

In 1903 a man named Henry Ford started a company in Detroit, Michigan, to **manufacture** cars. Manufacture means to make something using machines. Ford used an **assembly line**. On an assembly line, each worker performs a certain task. All the tasks together make the product. Using an assembly line made it faster and cheaper to produce goods. Henry Ford sold his first Model T car in 1908. It was cheap enough so many more people could afford to own one.

QUICK CHECK

Cause and Effect **What happened because of the assembly line?**

Check Understanding

1. **VOCABULARY** Make a drawing showing what each vocabulary word means.
   elevator   skyscraper   assembly line

2. **READING SKILL** Sequence Use your chart from page 86 to write a paragraph on how inventions changed daily life in the United States.

First
Next
Last

3. **Write About It** Write a paragraph to explain how transportation changed from 1830 through the early 1900s.

Local Connections
Your Community's History

Janet lives in Elkhart, Indiana. She wanted to learn about her town's history. So she interviewed an older resident to find out how her community has changed. Then she created a poster about early leaders and historic areas in her community.

Here are some ways you can learn about your town's past:

- Interview an older relative or neighbor who has lived in your community for a long time.

- Look in your school or local library or on the Internet for information about your community's history. Look at old newspapers and photos to see what your community looked like long ago.

- Make a time line of three or four key events in your community's history.

- Take photographs or draw sketches of older buildings or businesses in your community.

LOG ON For help with your project visit www.macmillanmh.com

History Activity

Conduct an Interview

1. Before your interview, prepare a list of questions.

2. Take notes during the interview. If you decide to tape your interview, ask permission first.

3. Write a report of your interview and what you learned about your town's history.

Materials
- notebook
- pencil or pen
- lined paper

Make a Poster

1. Gather the photos you found. Use these to draw pictures of older buildings. Arrange the drawings and your own photos on your poster board.

2. Use a marker to print labels for each building. Include the building's name, the year it was built, and what it is used for today.

3. Include a time line of important community events.

4. Share your poster with the class.

Materials
- notebook
- crayons
- poster board
- photos and drawings
- markers

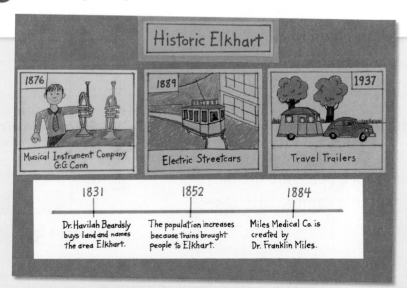

Historic Elkhart

1876 — Musical Instrument Company G.G. Conn
1889 — Electric Streetcars
1937 — Travel Trailers

1831 — Dr. Havilah Beardsly buys land and names the area Elkhart.

1852 — The population increases because trains brought people to Elkhart.

1884 — Miles Medical Co. is created by Dr. Franklin Miles.

Unit 2 Review and Assess

Vocabulary

Number a paper from 1 to 4. Beside each number write the word from the list below that matches the description.

settler   explorer

constitution   migration

1. a written plan of government

2. a person who makes a home in a new land

3. movement from one part of a country to another

4. a person who goes to a new place to find out about it

Comprehension and Critical Thinking

5. How did the Powhatan help settlers in Jamestown?

6. Reading Skill Why do immigrants often settle together in a community?

7. Critical Thinking How is travel today different from travel long ago?

8. Critical Thinking Why do people move to new places?

Skill

Use Bar Graphs

Look at the graph on the right. Write a complete sentence to answer each question.

9. What does this graph show?

10. Between 1890 and 1917, from which place did the most immigrants come?

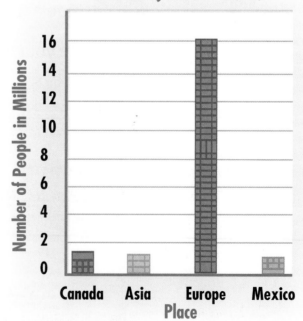

Immigration to the United States, 1890-1917

Test Preparation

Use the time line below to answer the questions.

Fighting for Freedom

1773 - The Boston Tea Party

1783 - Patriots win the American Revolution

| 1770 | 1775 | 1780 | 1785 | 1790 |

1776 - Declaration of Independence approved

1789 - George Washington becomes the first President of the United States

1. What is the first event on the time line?

A. Washington becomes President

B. Patriots win the revolution

C. the Boston Tea Party

D. the Declaration of Independence

2. How many years are between the Boston Tea Party and the war's end?

A. 16 years

B. 13 years

C. 10 years

D. 12 years

3. Which event happened after the American Revolution was won?

A. George Washington became President

B. The Boston Tea Party

C. The Declaration of Independence was written.

D. The Declaration of Independence was signed.

4. What do you think happened because of the Declaration of Independence?

How do communities change over time?

Write About the Big Idea

Descriptive Essay

In Unit 2 you read about how communities in the United States changed. Review the notes you made on your foldable. Begin your essay with a paragraph that states how communities changed over time.

Write one paragraph for each section of the foldable. Each paragraph should describe how communities were affected by the three topics.

Your final paragraph should summarize the main ideas of your essay.

Newcomers

Seeking Freedom

Inventions

Projects About the Big Idea

Make a Pictograph Find out the different ways of transportation that your classmates use to get to school. Make a pictograph that shows how many students use each type of transportation.

Write and Perform a Play You have read about traveling west on the Oregon Trail. Work in a small group to write a play about the pioneers' journey on the trail. Think of a problem a wagon train might have. Include the problem and the solution in your play. Perform your play for the class.

How We Get to School

car	
bus	
bicycle	
walking	

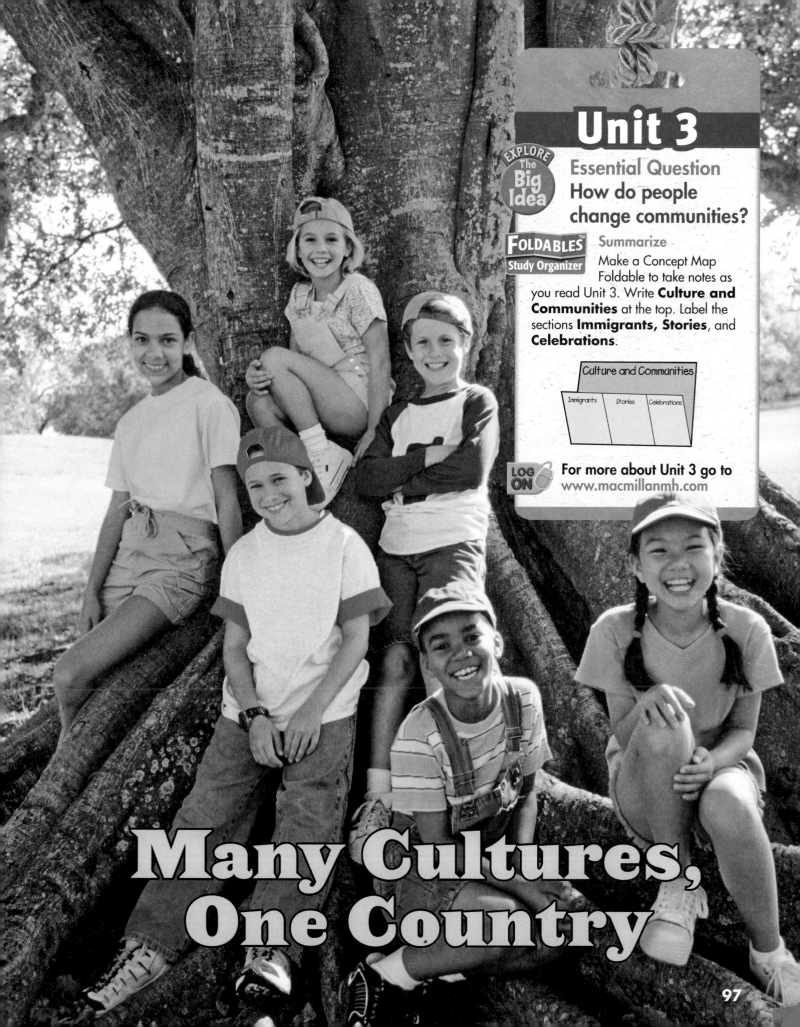

Unit 3

EXPLORE The Big Idea

Essential Question
How do people change communities?

FOLDABLES™
Study Organizer

Summarize
Make a Concept Map Foldable to take notes as you read Unit 3. Write **Culture and Communities** at the top. Label the sections **Immigrants, Stories**, and **Celebrations**.

Culture and Communities

| Immigrants | Stories | Celebrations |

LOG ON
For more about Unit 3 go to
www.macmillanmh.com

Many Cultures, One Country

PEOPLE, PLACES, AND EVENTS

W. Richard West, Jr.

National Museum of the American Indian

Opening ceremony

2004
Native Americans celebrate at the opening of the museum.

The **National Museum of the American Indian** in Washington, D.C., opened in 2004. The museum is run by **W. Richard West, Jr.**, a peace chief of the Southern Cheyenne.

Today you can visit the museum and learn about different Native American groups.

For more about People, Places, and Events, visit
www.macmillanmh.com

Flagler Street Gusman Center in Miami

Sweet Honey in the Rock

The group in concert

2006 | Sweet Honey in the Rock performs in Miami, Florida.

Sweet Honey in the Rock is a group of female African American singers. They sang at **Flagler Street Gusman Center in Miami**.

Today people can hear Sweet Honey in the Rock sing about freedom and equal rights.

A Land of Immigrants

VOCABULARY

custom p. 103

heritage p. 103

generation p. 103

READING SKILL

Summarize
Copy the chart. As you read, use it to summarize what happens when immigrants come to the United States.

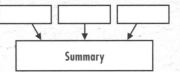

Summary

STANDARDS FOCUS

SOCIAL STUDIES — Global Connections

GEOGRAPHY — The Uses of Geography

Visual Preview

What happens when immigrants come to the United States?

A Immigrants come to the United States from many countries.

B Immigrants bring their culture and heritage with them.

C Immigrants face many new challenges in their new home.

D The immigrants' customs become part of their new community's culture.

COMING TO THE UNITED STATES

Maybe your family has stories about how they came to the United States. How was life here different from what they knew in their home country?

About 100 years ago, great numbers of immigrants came to the United States from Europe. Do you think that immigration was all in the past? Not at all! People still come here to make new homes every day. Today though, most immigrants come from Asia, Mexico, or Central America. Many also come from Africa and from islands in the Caribbean Sea.

▲ Central America lies between North and South America.

Immigrants all have one thing in common. No matter where they come from or when they first arrive in the United States, they all move to this country to find a better life. Some come for jobs or so their children can go to good schools. Others come to find freedom. All of them help the United States grow.

QUICK CHECK

Summarize Why do immigrants move to the United States?

As immigrants came to this country, the population of the United States grew. The Datagraphic below shows information about immigration and how it affected the population between 1950 and 2000.

DataGraphic

Immigration and Population

Study the pictograph and bar graph below. Answer the questions that follow.

Immigration to the United States, 1950–2000

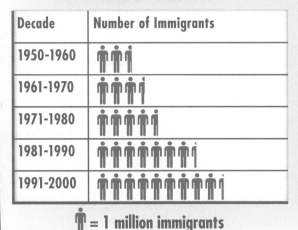

Decade	Number of Immigrants
1950-1960	
1961-1970	
1971-1980	
1981-1990	
1991-2000	

= 1 million immigrants

United States Population, 1950–2000

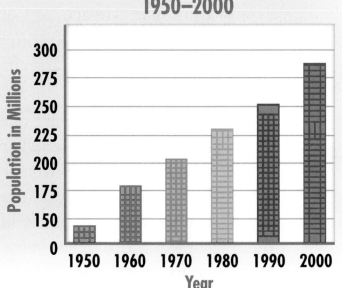

Think About Immigration and Population

1. In what year did the population of the United States first reach more than 200 million?

2. If the bar graph showed information for 2010, what do you think it would show?

Sharing Customs

Immigrants do more than add to the country's population—they bring new **customs**. A custom is a way of doing something that is shared by many people. Do you like to snack on chips and salsa? Not long ago most Americans did not eat these items. Immigrants from Mexico, like Maria's family, brought these things with them from Mexico.

Tacos

1 pound ground beef
1 chopped onion
2 chopped tomatoes
1 cup salsa
8 ounces cheese
8 warm tortillas

Cook beef and onions. Add the chopped tomatoes and salsa. Spoon 2 tablespoons of the cooked beef mixture onto each tortilla. Add some cheese. Roll or fold up the tortilla. Enjoy!

Maria's mother taught her how to make tacos because they are part of her family's **heritage**—something handed down from the past. The heritage that people share is passed from one **generation** to the next. A generation is a group of people born and living around the same time. Someday Maria will teach her children how to make tacos. Teaching something to the next generation is one way to keep a group's heritage alive.

When immigrants like Maria's family come to the United States, they share their customs with their new American friends. People come here from all over the world. They bring their customs and share them with the rest of us. This is how we all get to enjoy things like tacos that might not be part of our own family's heritage.

Maria helps her mother prepare tacos. ▼

QUICK CHECK

Main Idea and Details **How do Americans learn about the customs of other countries?**

C STARTING A NEW LIFE

Have you ever moved to a new place and had to start over to make friends? Was it difficult? Maybe you felt strange at first. Many immigrants feel that way when they first arrive in the United States. Living in a new place is a challenge! Many newcomers must learn to speak English. They must also learn their way around new neighborhoods, meet new people, and make new friends.

Think what it might be like if you couldn't read the street signs in your new neighborhood! ▶

◀ In Chau Lam's old school, all the students were Vietnamese.

"I was a stranger in a strange land. I'd never seen blonds or redheads before, never seen blue eyes or green. They couldn't understand me. I couldn't understand them. Yet, I realized, this was my new life."

Chau Lam (on the right, age 9)
Newspaper article
May 1, 2005

Write About It Write a paragraph describing how you felt on your first day of school. How is it similar to or different from how Chau Lam felt?

One Immigrant's Story

Chau Lam was 8 years old when she came from Vietnam, a country in Asia, to live in the United States. A war had just ended in her country—Chau Lam and her family were escaping to find a better life. They took a dangerous trip by boat. After many weeks they made their way safely to New York City. You can read above what Chau Lam remembers feeling about her first day of school in the United States.

Chau Lam's new classmates looked different from her classmates back in Vietnam. ▼

QUICK CHECK

Main Idea and Details
What are some challenges immigrants may face after coming to the United States?

Ada also came from another country to live in the United States. Ada was born in Nigeria, in West Africa. She had never seen a paved road, used an elevator, or eaten pizza! When she moved to Crownsville, Maryland, she experienced all of these strange new things.

When Ada came to Crownsville, she joined a community where other people from Nigeria were already living. This helped her feel at home as she got to know American culture. At the local market, she could buy Nigerian clothing and food. She also shared her customs with others in her community who were not familiar with Nigerian culture. People in Ada's community loved learning about her culture—and Ada enjoyed learning about other cultures, too.

◀ Kente is a colorful cloth from Africa.

These girls open a coconut at a Nigerian festival in Crownsville, Maryland.

Playing drums at the Nigerian festival

▲ These young people are dressed in Nigerian clothing.

A Mixed Culture

In the United States, we learn from immigrants from other countries. That is how culture in the United States developed. American culture is like a stew of many ingredients! Over time the customs of many different immigrant groups have been added to the culture we all share today.

QUICK CHECK

Summarize **Why do immigrants sometimes live in communities with people from their home country?**

Check Understanding

1. **VOCABULARY** Use the vocabulary words below to write a letter to an older relative.

   custom   heritage   generation

2. **READING SKILL** Summarize Use your chart from page 100 to summarize what happens when immigrants come to the United States.

3. **Write About It** Write a paragraph that tells how a community shares customs.

107

Lesson 2

VOCABULARY

ethnic group p. 109

diverse p. 109

architecture p. 110

READING SKILL

Summarize
Copy the chart below. As
you read, list things that
make up a culture.

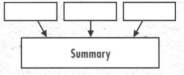

STANDARDS FOCUS

| SOCIAL STUDIES | Culture |
| GEOGRAPHY | Places and Regions |

All About Culture

Girls dancing the
hula in Hawaii

Visual Preview

How have other cultures become part of American culture?

A New people
bring their
cultures when they
immigrate.

B Artists may
borrow some
ideas from other
cultures.

C Musicians make
new types of
music when cultures
mix.

D Dances from
many cultures
are enjoyed in the
United States.

A LAND OF MANY CULTURES

You wake up and pull on your favorite jeans. You pour a bowl of cereal while you listen to your favorite music. Clothes, food, and music are all part of your culture.

By 2003 there were more than 33 million people living in the United States who were not born here. These people came here from other countries. They are from many different **ethnic groups**. An ethnic group is a group of people who share the same language and culture. People in every ethnic group bring their customs with them when they immigrate. The things different ethnic groups brought have helped make the United States a very **diverse**, or varied, land.

Some customs are brought to the United States by immigrants. Other customs are created right here. Together these customs from near and far mix and make one big, rich culture that we all share. In fact, the United States has one of the most diverse cultures on Earth!

QUICK CHECK

Summarize Why is United States culture so diverse?

These instruments come from countries in Asia and Africa. ▶

109

PAINTING AND ARCHITECTURE

Everywhere you look you can see how other cultures have added to American culture. This is especially true of things like painting and **architecture**. Architecture is the art of designing buildings. Artists often look to other cultures for ideas to use in their work. Here are two examples.

In the United States

African American artist Jacob Lawrence made a group of paintings about the Great Migration—the journey of African Americans who moved from the South to the North and Midwest in the early to mid-1900s. Where did Lawrence get his ideas?

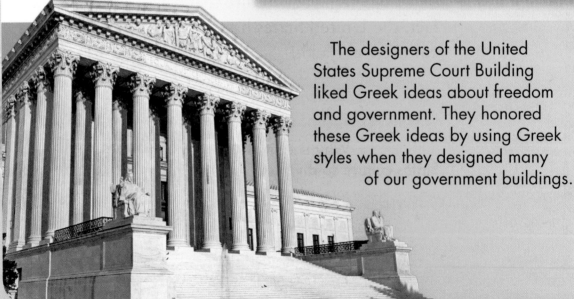

The designers of the United States Supreme Court Building liked Greek ideas about freedom and government. They honored these Greek ideas by using Greek styles when they designed many of our government buildings.

The ideas that artists borrow become part of their art. If you go to a museum to look at Jacob Lawrence's paintings, or if you visit the United States Supreme Court Building, you will see different ideas that are now part of American culture.

QUICK CHECK

Main Idea and Details **What kinds of ideas are borrowed from other places and cultures?**

Around the World

African art often uses flat shapes and bright colors, as in this painting. Lawrence borrowed these ideas and made them part of his work. This is one way African ideas became part of American culture.

The Parthenon was built in Greece thousands of years ago. Huge columns carved from stone hold up the roof. What ideas do you think the designers of the Supreme Court building borrowed from the Parthenon? How are the buildings similar?

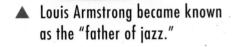

Every country and culture has its own special music. When people move from one place to another, they bring the music they love with them. Africans who came to the United States brought their songs and rhythms with them. Louis Armstrong and other musicians changed the African music and turned it into jazz—a new and exciting American music. Jazz, blues, and ragtime are all kinds of music that grew out of African music.

▲ Louis Armstrong became known as the "father of jazz."

Sweet Honey in the Rock, or "Sweet Honey," is a group of six African American women who sing African songs with African rhythms. They also sing American songs—spirituals and songs about freedom and equal rights.

EVENT

The **Harlem Renaissance** was a time of great creativity that took place in the 1920s in Harlem in New York City. African American writers, artists, and musicians used their work to share African American culture.

Harlem in the 1920s

North America's First Sport

Sports are an important part of a group's culture. Lacrosse was probably North America's first sport. Native Americans created it hundreds of years ago. They used the game to help settle arguments. In 1636 French settlers in Canada saw the game. Soon they began playing lacrosse, too. In the 1800s new rules were added to the game, and lacrosse became more popular.

Lacrosse has changed a lot since the Native Americans played! It is now a combination of basketball, soccer, and hockey. Each player carries a crosse—a stick with a net on the end. The crosse is used to throw, catch, or scoop a ball off a grass field and into the goal.

▲ Native American lacrosse teams often had hundreds of players on a side.

Today more than 100,000 high school students play lacrosse.

QUICK CHECK

Summarize How did jazz and lacrosse become part of American culture?

113

Ⓓ DANCE

Dance is an important part of culture. Music and dance go together! In Mexico many villages have their own special dances. Mexicans brought these dances with them to the United States and passed them on to their children as part of their heritage.

Many dances are part of holiday celebrations. Chinese boys often learn the dragon dance or the fan dance to celebrate New Year.

▲ Chinese boys dance to celebrate the Chinese New Year.

QUICK CHECK

Main Idea How are dances part of a culture?

▲ Dancers celebrating Cinco de Mayo.

Check Understanding

1. **VOCABULARY** Write one sentence for each vocabulary term below.
   ethnic group   **diverse**   **architecture**

2. **READING SKILL**
   Summarize Use your chart from page 108 to write a paragraph that summarizes the things that are part of culture.

 3. **Write About It** Write a paragraph that tells how people in a community learn about different cultures.

Citizenship

Points of View

Should old buildings be torn down?

What should we do with old buildings? Do we need them? Read three points of view on whether old buildings should be saved.

Michigan
New York
Ohio

"It's not good to tear down old buildings. We have a building nearby that was President Theodore Roosevelt's house. We saw what it was like to live back then. We wouldn't have been able to do that if the building was gone."

Halle
Commack, New York
From an interview, 2006

"Some old buildings should be torn down. There is an old rundown building in our city. It doesn't look nice. It would cost too much money to fix it up. Maybe a park could go in its place."

Jordan
Detroit, Michigan
From an interview, 2006

"Historical old buildings should be saved. If the building cannot be saved just as it is, some special parts of the building should be saved so that it can go somewhere like a museum. Buildings people think of as American, like the White House, should definitely be saved."

Jose
Cleveland, Ohio
From an interview, 2006

Write About It Write a paragraph about a building in your community that you think should be saved.

Sharing Culture Through Stories

VOCABULARY

hero p. 117

value p. 117

READING SKILL

Summarize
Copy the chart below. As you read, list information about stories from different cultures. Then write a summary statement.

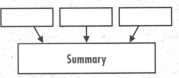

Summary

STANDARDS FOCUS

SOCIAL STUDIES — Culture

GEOGRAPHY — Places and Regions

Visual Preview

Why are stories important to a culture?

A Stories are a way of sharing the important ideas of a culture.

B Myths and fables help explain important beliefs.

C Legends help tell us what is important to a culture.

D Some stories teach us about some qualities of our leaders.

Where did mountains come from? Why is the grass green? People in the past weren't sure how to answer these questions. So they told stories to explain the answers.

Some stories from the past are about **heroes**. A hero is someone you admire because of his or her achievements or personal qualities. These stories have been passed down over many generations. There are different kinds of stories, but they all teach us about the beliefs and **values** of a culture. A value is an idea—like honesty or courage—that people in a culture care about and think important. By listening to these stories we can learn about our own culture and other cultures as well.

This Native American doll shows a storyteller surrounded by children. ▼

We can tell stories, too. We can share stories we have heard from others, or we can tell stories of our own that have never been told before. No matter what kind of story is told, people can share their culture with others through stories. In this lesson you'll read about stories that are part of different cultures.

QUICK CHECK

Summarize What can we learn by listening to stories?

117

B MYTHS AND FABLES

People from many cultures all over the world tell stories called myths. A myth can tell about or explain a belief shared by a group of people. Some myths are about heroes or gods and goddesses. Many myths explain how something came to be in nature or how a custom got started. A lot of myths use animals to explain things.

The Hopi—a Native American group that live in the southwestern United States—have a myth to explain where stars came from. In "How Coyote Placed the Stars," animals help make the world and put the rivers, mountains, and forests in their places. Read the story below to see what happened next.

"How Coyote Placed the Stars"

Long ago the animals helped make the world. The birds wanted to decorate the desert, so they gathered hundreds of small shiny rocks into a large pile. When they went home to sleep, Coyote crept from his hiding place to investigate. When he found the rocks were not good to eat, he took them one by one and threw them up into the sky. They still shine there today.

Stories With a Lesson

People everywhere have told stories for thousands of years. Over time, different stories from cultures around the world have become part of our American culture, too.

One type of story is called a fable. A fable is a short story that teaches a moral or lesson. In fables the characters are usually animals that talk and act just like people.

Aesop's Fables

A man named Aesop lived in Greece long ago. He was enslaved, but he was so good at telling stories that he earned his freedom by telling a story. Eventually he became famous for his fables.

One of Aesop's best known fables is "The Fox and the Grapes." Read this fable on the right of the page. Do you know anyone who acts like this fox? Like all fables, this one teaches us a lesson.

QUICK CHECK

Main Idea and Details **What do you think the story on this page is trying to teach?**

"The Fox and the Grapes"

A hungry Fox saw a bunch of fat, juicy grapes hanging from a tall vine. She jumped and jumped but could not reach them. She tried all her tricks but it was no use. Tired and still hungry, she finally gave up. As the Fox trotted away she sniffed, "Who cares? Those grapes were sour anyway!"

Not all stories told in our country come from somewhere else. The Paul Bunyan stories are American—they weren't borrowed or passed down from another culture the way Aesop's fables were. Like myths and fables, they can tell us something about the values of a culture.

Stories about Paul Bunyan were first told around campfires by real-life lumberjacks. They were told to entertain. The stories are actually a special kind of story called a tall tale. In a tall tale, many details are exaggerated, or "larger than life."

Paul's Adventures

Paul Bunyan was a make-believe person who was more than 50 feet tall! He became famous for his size, strength, and skill at clearing forests. Some stories include Bunyan's best friend, Babe, a blue ox that was as big as a mountain. The people who told these stories exaggerated the skills important to lumberjacks.

According to one story, Bunyan traveled across the country, clearing forests so pioneers could plant crops and build villages, houses, bridges, barns, and ships. One day he dragged his ax behind him and left a big ditch in his tracks. That was how the Grand Canyon was made!

PLACES

These statues of Paul Bunyan and Babe stand in **Bemidji, Minnesota**. According to one story, Minnesota's 10,000 lakes—including Lake Bemidji—were made from Paul and Babe's footsteps.

Bemidji, Minnesota

Once Bunyan started a logging camp. He hired 1,000 men who were each more than 10 feet tall. Bunyan needed to make sure all these men had enough to eat and drink. Read below to find out what Paul did.

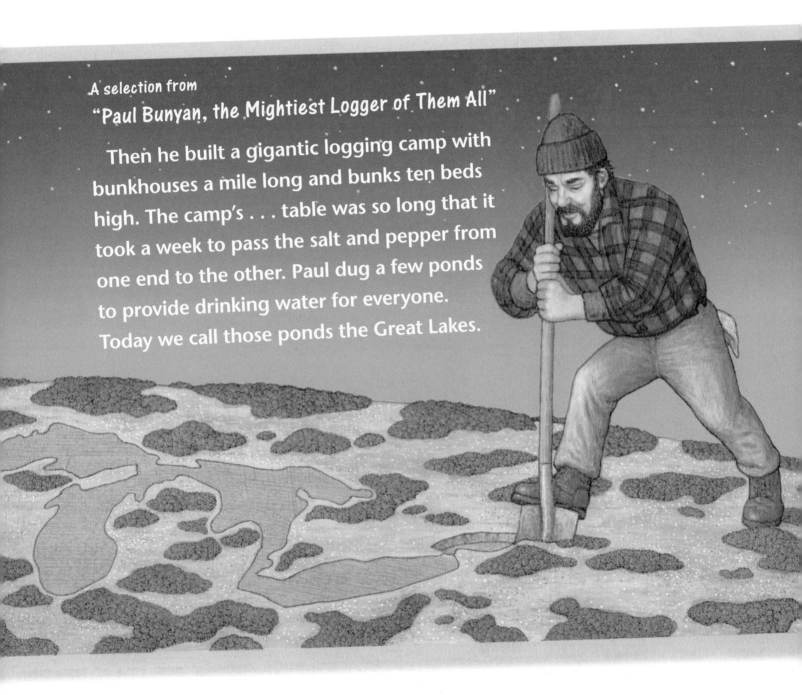

A selection from
"Paul Bunyan, the Mightiest Logger of Them All"

Then he built a gigantic logging camp with bunkhouses a mile long and bunks ten beds high. The camp's . . . table was so long that it took a week to pass the salt and pepper from one end to the other. Paul dug a few ponds to provide drinking water for everyone. Today we call those ponds the Great Lakes.

QUICK CHECK

Summarize **Why do you think the lumberjacks told the Paul Bunyan stories?**

Ⓓ LEARNING FROM A LEGEND

A legend is a story based on something that really happened, or on the life of a real person. The story has been added to over time, though, so it is not entirely true. Some legends are about heroes. Since heroes are people we admire, sharing stories about heroes is a way we teach others to be like our heroes.

An American Hero

Many Americans believe George Washington is a hero because he was such a great leader. On the next page you can read part of an American legend about George Washington.

From

"The Life of Washington" by Mason L. Weems

"George," said his father, "do you know who killed that beautiful little cherry-tree yonder in the garden?" . . . [George] bravely cried out, "I can't tell a lie, Pa; you know I can't tell a lie. I did cut it with my hatchet. . . ." "Run to my arms, you dearest boy," cried his father. . . . "Such an act of heroism [telling the truth] in my son, is [of] more worth than a thousand trees. . . ."

This story never really happened. Then why was it written? Because it helps us understand something about Washington—that he was an honest person. Honesty is an important quality for leaders to have. Stories like this are supposed to help us learn about heroes and leaders and want to be like them.

QUICK CHECK

Summarize **What does the legend about George Washington teach us?**

Check Understanding

1. **VOCABULARY** Use the words below to write a description of a hero.
   hero   **value**

2. **READING SKILL**
   Summarize Use your chart from page 116 to summarize what stories can teach us.

3. **Write About It** Write a paragraph to explain why people tell stories about heroes.

Local Celebrations

VOCABULARY

founder p. 125

holiday p. 130

READING SKILL

Summarize
Copy the chart below. Use it to summarize what communities celebrate.

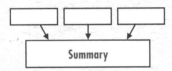

Summary

STANDARDS FOCUS

SOCIAL STUDIES   Individual Development and Identity

GEOGRAPHY   Places and Regions

Children dress like Tom Sawyer and Becky Thatcher for National Tom Sawyer Days.

Visual Preview

What are some reasons communities celebrate?

A Communities celebrate both important and fun parts of their culture.

B Some places celebrate with county fairs to honor what people can do.

C Communities all over the world celebrate their nation's independence.

D Some Native Americans hold powwows to honor their heritage.

CELEBRATING COMMUNITIES

Welcome to Hannibal, Missouri. Today is the day of the frog jumping contest at National Tom Sawyer Days. We set our frogs down at the starting line. They're off!

People in Hannibal, Missouri, celebrate National Tom Sawyer Days to honor the writer Mark Twain. Tom Sawyer was a character in one of Twain's books. People in Hannibal are proud of Mark Twain.

Barbourville, Kentucky, has a Daniel Boone Festival. Daniel Boone was the town's **founder**. A founder is a person who starts something, such as a business or a town. At the festival people enjoy events like a carnival, an art show, and a parade. Some even dress up like Daniel Boone!

Celebrating Food

Communities celebrate for many reasons. In some places food is the reason! People in Barnesville, Minnesota, celebrate a Potato Days festival every year. The potato is important to their community's culture. They have a parade, races, and even a "dress-the-potato" contest!

▼ Will this frog win the frog jumping contest?

QUICK CHECK

Summarize **Why do communities celebrate certain people?**

125

Almost every community celebrates something. Across the country, people celebrate things we all have in common. For example, people in many towns plant and care for trees on Arbor Day. Many communities celebrate a Founder's Day, too.

Some communities celebrate by holding a county fair every year. In Goshen, Indiana, people enjoy the Elkhart County 4-H Fair. What is 4-H? It is an organization for young people between the ages of 5 and 19. Young people learn lots of skills in 4-H. They learn to raise animals and care for plants, and how to help their community. County fairs are often held by 4-H groups to celebrate young people and their accomplishments.

▲ At county fairs children often show off the animals they have raised. Some will win a blue ribbon!

Some communities celebrate their pets with a parade.

Celebrating Children

More and more communities are celebrating El Día de los Niños, El Día de los Libros. That is Spanish for Children's Day, Book Day. The first celebrations took place at libraries in Arizona, New Mexico, and Texas. Now Children's Day is celebrated all over the country. If you like to read, this is the celebration for you. On this day children enjoy a parade, free books, gifts, music, and games.

▲ The power of books is celebrated on Children's Day, Book Day.

QUICK CHECK

Main Idea and Details **What are some ways communities celebrate young people?**

PEOPLE

Pat Mora writes children's books. In 1996 Mora learned that in Mexico, April 30 is Children's Day, or Día de Los Niños. Mora decided to start Children's Day, Book Day in the United States as a way to share books.

Pat Mora

127

C AMERICANS CELEBRATE FREEDOM

It's hard to believe there was ever a time when Americans weren't free. Americans celebrate the idea of freedom because it is so important to us. On Veteran's Day we celebrate all those who have served in the armed forces. Memorial Day is a time for us to remember those who died fighting for our country.

Some towns hold parades on the Fourth of July. ▼

Independence Day

Americans celebrate our independence from Great Britain on the Fourth of July, also known as Independence Day. We call it America's birthday. Many Americans celebrate with parades, fireworks, picnics, and concerts.

Communities celebrate the Fourth in different ways. Seward, Alaska, has a foot race. Lititz, Pennsylvania, has a Festival of Candles. How does your community celebrate Independence Day?

The United States is not the only country to celebrate independence. Read the next page to see how people in India celebrate their Independence Day.

QUICK CHECK

Main Idea and Details **How do Americans celebrate the idea of freedom?**

Global Connections

Independence in India

India is a large country in Asia. India celebrates its independence on August 15. Like people in the United States, people in India celebrate freedom from British rule. On Independence Day the Indian flag is raised in cities and towns all over India. The flag flies over government buildings in New Delhi, India's capital city. Students in schools raise the flag in special ceremonies.

Another popular activity on Independence Day in India is kite flying. Indian children fly kites of all shapes, colors, and sizes to celebrate their country's independence.

Young people love to wear the colors of India to celebrate Independence Day.

India

Write About It Suppose you were planning an Independence Day celebration. Write a paragraph describing the activities you would include in your celebration.

CELEBRATING HERITAGE

A **holiday** is a day on which we honor important heroes and special events by celebrating. These heroes and events are part of our heritage. Americans celebrate many different holidays.

Martin Luther King, Jr., Day is a holiday for all Americans. King was a hero who fought for equal rights. Other holidays celebrate events from our country's history. People in some states celebrate Juneteenth—June 19, 1865, the day slavery ended in Texas. Some African Americans think of Juneteenth as their independence day. Thanksgiving Day started with the Pilgrims in Plymouth, Massachusetts. We celebrate it today as a day to give thanks.

▲ Members of a girl's dance team celebrate Juneteenth in Austin, Texas.

▲ Juneteenth became an official state holiday in Texas in 1980.

▲ Community marching bands are a highlight of the parade.

◀ Children dance at powwows.

Sharing Heritage

People from many ethnic groups have special days. Mexicans celebrate Cinco de Mayo—the fifth of May. On this day in 1862 the Mexican army won an important battle against the French.

Some Native Americans honor their culture by holding powwows. A powwow is a gathering with dancing and music. The dancers sometimes compete against each other. The National Museum of the American Indian in Washington, D.C., sponsors a powwow in August each year.

QUICK CHECK

Sequence What events in history were later honored by holidays?

Check Understanding

1. **VOCABULARY** Write one sentence for each vocabulary word below.
   founder **holiday**

2. **READING SKILL** Summarize Use your chart from page 124 to write a paragraph that summarizes the reasons communities celebrate.

 3. Write About It Choose a day your community celebrates. Write a description of how your community celebrates this day.

Cultures Around the World

VOCABULARY

tradition p.133

ancestor p.133

READING SKILL

Summarize
Copy the chart below. As you read, use it to summarize ways cultures celebrate.

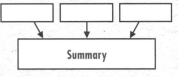

Summary

STANDARDS FOCUS

SOCIAL STUDIES Culture

GEOGRAPHY Human Systems

Dancers in Ghana celebrate the yam festival.

Visual Preview

What are some ways cultures around the world celebrate?

A Food is an important part of many cultural celebrations.

B Some cultural celebrations include special dances.

C Some cultures use puppets at festivals to tell stories.

A FESTIVALS AND FOOD

The Chinese Moon Festival celebrates the full moon at harvest time. People in China eat mooncakes during this festival. What do you think mooncakes look like?

Like mooncakes, some foods are a special part of celebrations. Is there a food your family always has for a holiday? Then it is a **tradition**. A tradition is a way of doing something that is passed along by family members over many years. Cultural traditions include foods, music, dances, and other arts.

Celebrating With Food

In the last lesson, you read about a potato festival in our country. Ghana is a country in West Africa that has a celebration called the yam festival. Yams are a very important crop in Ghana. During the festival people sing and dance to celebrate.

In Mexico people celebrate the Day of the Dead, or El Día de los Muertos. On this day Mexicans remember their **ancestors**. Ancestors are early members of your family who have died, such as great-grandparents. The meal at this celebration often includes pan de muerto, or bread of the dead.

▼ Bread made for a Day of the Dead celebration

QUICK CHECK

Summarize Tell some ways food is part of cultural celebrations.

Dancers doing a reel

B DANCING AT CELEBRATIONS

Jump up high and kick your legs out to the sides. Be sure to keep your back straight and to point your toes. These are steps in a highland dance from Scotland called the reel. Most highland dances are hard to do—they take a lot of strength and have very difficult movements.

Highland Games

Some communities in Scotland hold celebrations called highland games. These celebrations started in a mountainous area of northern Scotland called the Highlands. Highland games include competitions in dancing. Dancing is part of Scottish culture.

The Scottish tradition of highland dancing has become part of American culture as well. Groups like the Celtic Society of Southern Maryland and the Caledonian Club of San Francisco, California, hold contests in highland dancing.

▲ Girls doing the Sword Dance

A Chinese Dance

You can hear the drums. A large dragon winds its way down the street. It looks like the dragon is dancing! You must be at a Chinese New Year parade. Why is a dragon dance part of the celebration? In China the dragon is a symbol of luck and success. People once performed the dragon dance to please the dragon and to ask it for rain during dry times.

A team of dancers carries a dragon made of bamboo, silk, and paper. The dragon could be as much as 100 feet long! The dancers use poles to lift the dragon up and down to the sound of a thumping drum. Today people enjoy watching the dancers perform this tradition at many Chinese celebrations.

▼ These boys work hard to hold up their dragon.

QUICK CHECK

Compare and Contrast How are the reel and the dragon dance alike?

The dragon dance is a traditional Chinese dance. ▼

135

PUPPETS AROUND THE WORLD

Have you ever made a puppet or put on a puppet show? Many festivals around the world have puppet shows especially for children. Puppets can be part of a country's culture.

Types of Puppets

If you have ever seen your shadow, you have an idea how puppet shows in Indonesia work. Indonesia is a country in Asia. Shadow puppets are popular there. The puppets are made of buffalo or goatskin that is cut into large figures. They are held in front of a light. The audience watches the puppets' shadows on a screen. The puppets tell a traditional story about good and evil.

In England children enjoy Punch and Judy shows. These puppets fit over the hand.

◀ Indonesian shadow puppets

Children watch a puppet show in England. ▼

"Punch" is a hand puppet.

PROFESSOR
M. POULTON
proudly presents the
PUNCH & JUDY
SHOW

Calliacombeton
Sands
Prof. Mark Poulton

brighton

136   Lesson 5

▲ Marionettes in a museum in Italy

Marionettes are puppets that are moved by pulling strings. The name marionette comes from France, but these puppets are used in Italy, too, another country in Europe. In the photo above, even the musicians are puppets! Traditional Italian puppet shows sometimes tell a story about knights in history. Which type of puppet show would you enjoy watching the most?

QUICK CHECK

Main Idea and Details **What are some different kinds of puppets?**

Check Understanding

1. **VOCABULARY** Write one sentence for each of the vocabulary words below.
   tradition   **ancestor**

2. **READING SKILL** Summarize
   Use your chart from page
   132 to write a paragraph
   about ways cultures celebrate.

3. **Write About It** Write a letter to a friend about a cultural celebration you have enjoyed.

Map and Globe Skills
Understand Latitude and Longitude

VOCABULARY

grid

latitude

longitude

degree

Every place on Earth has an address, which tells its exact location. To describe the location of a place, geographers use maps with **grids**. Grids are lines that cross each other on a map. Earth's grid has two sets of lines called **latitude** and **longitude**.

Lines of latitude measure how far north or south a place is from the equator. Lines of longitude measure distance east or west of the prime meridian. Lines of latitude and longitude measure distance on Earth's surface in **degrees**. The symbol for degrees is °.

Learn It

- Look at Map A. Lines of latitude north of the equator are labeled **N**. Lines of latitude south of the equator are labeled **S**.

- Now look at Map B. Lines of longitude east of the prime meridian are labeled **E**. Lines of longitude west of the prime meridian are labeled **W**.

- Lines of latitude and lines of longitude can be used to locate any place on Earth. When you locate places on a map, give the latitude first and longitude second.

Map A

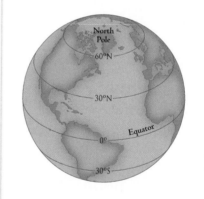

Map B

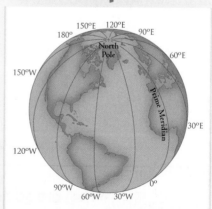

Try It

Use Map C below to answer the questions.

- What line of latitude is at 0 degrees?

- Is Sydney east or west of the prime meridian?

Apply It

- Give the closest latitude and longitude address of Cairo, Egypt.

- Which city is nearest to the address of 30°S, 60°W?

- Find the latitude and longitude closest to San Francisco.

Map C

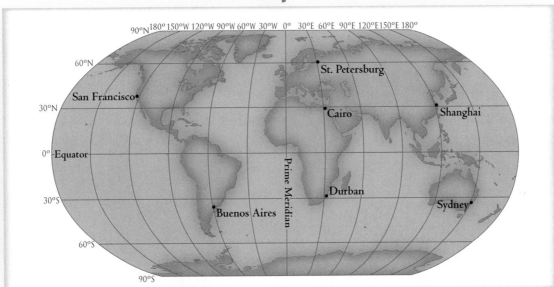

Local Connections

Food in Your Community

Sam lives in Jersey City, New Jersey. He wanted to show what he had learned about some of the ethnic groups in his community. So he created a menu for a restaurant that would serve foods from many ethnic groups. Here are steps you can follow to do the same thing.

- Use your library or the Internet to find out about the ethnic groups that live in your community. Find out what types of foods are popular in each of these cultures. Make copies of recipes and photos of different ethnic foods.

- Sam made a menu for his restaurant. He decorated a cover for the menu and listed the menu items on the inside. On the front cover, he wrote the name of his restaurant. He called it "Foods from Around the World."

LOG ON For more help with your project visit
www.macmillanmh.com

Cultural Activity

Make a Menu

1 Gather your notes and photos.

2 Make a menu for your community's new restaurant. Use markers or colored pencils to make drawings of menu items based on your photos.

3 Decorate the front cover of your menu. Include the name of your restaurant on the cover.

4 Share your menu with the class.

Materials
- construction paper
- white paper
- markers
- crayons
- colored pencils

Unit 3 Review and Assess

Vocabulary

Write a sentence or more to answer each question. Use the vocabulary words in your sentences.

1. Describe a **custom** your family has.
2. Explain what **architecture** is.
3. Tell something you do to celebrate your favorite **holiday**.
4. Tell which countries your **ancestors** came from.

Comprehension and Critical Thinking

5. Why are stories important?
6. Why do Americans celebrate Independence Day?
7. Reading Skill Why would an immigrant join a community of people who came from the same place that he or she did?
8. Critical Thinking Why is it important to learn about customs and celebrations in other cultures?

Skill

Understand Latitude and Longitude

Write a complete sentence to answer each question.

9. Which city is closest to 40 °N, 89 °W?
10. What is the latitude and longitude "address" closest to Galesburg?

Illinois: Latitude and Longitude

Test Preparation

Read the paragraph. Answer the questions.

> The Chinese New Year usually lasts fifteen days. On the first day—New Year's Day—children receive red envelopes called Lai-See. The envelopes have money inside and are given for good luck. On the seventh day farmers display their crops. The seventh day is also called "everybody's birthday." On the last day there is a Lantern Festival. On that night people carry lanterns into the street for a parade. The best part of the Lantern Festival parade is the dragon dance. This popular dance is a great way to end the celebration!

1. When does the Lantern Festival take place?

   A. on the seventh day

   B. on the first day

   C. on the fifteenth day

   D. all fifteen days

2. What is the paragraph mostly about?

   A. Lai-See envelopes

   B. Lantern Festival

   C. everybody's birthday

   D. Chinese New Year

3. How do you think children feel when they are given Lai-See envelopes?

4. What are some ways other cultures celebrate the new year?

The Big Idea Activities

How do people change communities?

Write About the Big Idea

Narrative Essay

Use the Unit 3 foldable to help you write a narrative essay that answers the Big Idea question, "How do people change communities?" Begin with a topic sentence. Use the notes you wrote on the foldable to include details about ways people change communities. End with a paragraph that summarizes your essay and answers the question.

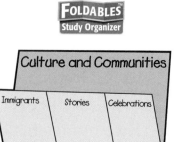

FOLDABLES™ Study Organizer

Culture and Communities

| Immigrants | Stories | Celebrations |

Projects About the Big Idea

Make a Poster Make a poster that shows food, stories, art, dance, and sports that are part of your culture.

Make a Map You have read about cultural celebrations around the world. Work with a partner to make a map that shows where these different celebrations take place. Make drawings that represent each celebration. Include your drawings on the map. Label each celebration and its location.

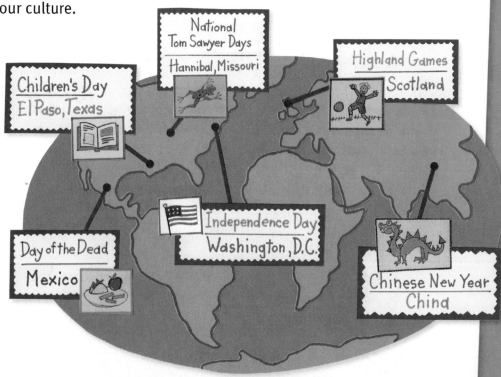

National Tom Sawyer Days
Hannibal, Missouri

Children's Day
El Paso, Texas

Highland Games
Scotland

Independence Day
Washington, D.C.

Day of the Dead
Mexico

Chinese New Year
China

EXPLORE The Big Idea

Essential Question
How do people in a community meet their needs?

FOLDABLES™
Study Organizer

Cause and Effect
Make a three-tab book foldable to take notes as you read Unit 4. Write the words **Meeting Needs** at the top.

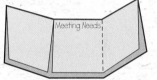

Meeting Needs

LOG ON

For more about Unit 4 go to
www.macmillanmh.com

Communities at Work

PEOPLE, PLACES, AND EVENTS

Louisiana Crafts Guild

New Orleans, Louisiana

Completed Home

2005

Workers in the Louisiana Crafts Guild helped to rebuild this house. It was once the home of jazz musician Red Allen.

The **Louisiana Crafts Guild** was created to teach young people construction skills needed to repair buildings.

Today students and builders work to fix old buildings in **New Orleans, Louisiana** that are damaged or falling down.

Henry Ford

Henry Ford Museum, Dearborn, Michigan

Factory Workers

1913 | Workers on an assembly line at the Ford Motor Company put together a car.

Henry Ford was the owner of a car company. Starting in 1913, Ford began using an **assembly line** to make cars quickly.

Today you can see and learn about Ford's cars at the **Henry Ford Museum** in Dearborn, Michigan.

Businesses in the Community

Lesson 1

VOCABULARY

employee p. 149

producer p. 150

consumer p. 150

profit p. 151

economy p. 152

READING SKILL

Cause and Effect

Copy the chart below. List the things that cause prices to go up or down.

Cause	→	Effect
	→	
	→	
	→	

STANDARDS FOCUS

SOCIAL STUDIES Production, Distribution, and Consumption

GEOGRAPHY Human Systems

Businesses help supply many needs in a town.

Visual Preview

How do people and businesses make money?

A People work at many different jobs to earn money.

B Farmers sell their crops to buyers for money.

C Businesses buy from other businesses to supply needs.

D Most people use money to pay for needs and wants.

A PEOPLE EARN MONEY

What jobs do people have? Doctors, plumbers, sales people—there are so many different jobs. Some people work outdoors, while others work in an office or a factory.

Almost everyone works at some kind of job. People work to earn money for all the things they need, such as food, clothing, and shelter. They work to have money for fun things like vacations, too. People also work because they enjoy what they do. Working at a job you really like is fun!

Most people work for someone else. They are **employees**. An employee is a person who gets paid to work for someone else—a company or a person—called an employer.

Think about a grocery store. A grocery store is a private business. Who orders the food and puts it on the shelves? Who puts up the price signs? Employees, of course! The owner or manager of the store hires people to do these and other jobs. The owner pays the employees a salary for their work.

QUICK CHECK

Cause and Effect **Why do people work?**

Many people work as doctors or nurses. ▶

Farmers like Mr. Smith are **producers**. A producer makes, grows, or supplies goods or services. Goods are something people buy, like apples.

Mr. Smith needs money to run his farm. He has to buy tall ladders, trucks, and boxes. Then he has to pay employees to pick the apples, put them in boxes, and load them onto trucks.

B SELLING THINGS FOR MONEY

Who grows or makes the things people buy? The apples, pumpkins, lettuce, and carrots sold at a farmers' market are grown on farms. Farmers sell the goods they grow. A farmer might sell a bag of apples for $4.00. How does a farmer decide on a price? The price needs to be high enough so that the farmer can pay for the things he needs to run the business—tools, equipment, and the employees needed to grow the apples.

A farmer also listens to **consumers** when deciding how much to charge. A consumer is a person who buys goods or uses a service. If consumers think a price is too high, they might not buy the product. Then the farmer might decide to lower the price so more people will buy.

Selling Price	$4.00
− Cost of Growing	$3.00
(tools, equipment, employees)	
= Profit	$1.00

Farmers sell their goods to make a **profit**. Profit is money a business makes after paying for tools, employees, and other costs. At the farmers' market, Mr. Smith has competition—other farmers who are selling apples.

Mr. Smith uses some of his profit to pay for more things he needs for the farm. But he can also use some of it to buy his son a new guitar!

Consumers Decide

Many farmers sell apples. If you are the seller, what can you do to get people to buy from you? You could advertise. You could grow a kind of apple that no one else sells. You might even shine all your apples so they look attractive and people will want to buy them.

What if you are the consumer? How do you decide where to buy an apple? Maybe you will buy from the seller with the lowest price. Perhaps you will buy from a farmer you know and trust. If you do not want to walk very far, you might buy from the closest market.

QUICK CHECK

Summarize How does a seller decide how much to charge?

Think of some things you will use today. Do you picture clothes, food, books, and pencils? These things probably come from stores in your community. These stores are part of your community's **economy**. The economy is the way a place uses its money, goods, natural resources, and services.

Sometimes a community needs goods and services from another community. Restaurants in New York City might depend on farmers in Washington or California to grow fresh ingredients for their meals. The farmers also depend on the restaurants to buy their fruits and vegetables. The two communities are interdependent. Their economies depend on each other. Countries buy and sell from one another as well.

QUICK CHECK

Cause and Effect **Why are some communities interdependent?**

WASHINGTON

New York City

▲ Food grown in Washington state is served in New York City.

Global Connections

A Dollar in Canada

Canada is an independent nation in North America. It has its own money. Canadian coins are made in the same values as United States coins—one cent, five cents, ten cents, twenty-five cents, and fifty cents.

Canada

Canada also has a dollar—but there is no dollar bill in Canada. In Canada, the dollar is a coin only. There is even a two-dollar coin. If you want to use paper money in Canada, you would need to trade five Canadian dollar coins for a Canadian five-dollar bill!

Canadian dollar ▼

When people or businesses in different countries buy and sell to one another, they use different kinds of money. For example, Mexico's money is called the peso. Russia's money is the ruble. The Japanese pay for things with yen.

United States dollar ▼

▲ Japanese yen

▲ Russian ruble

▲ Mexican peso

Write About It Write a paragraph describing how Canadian money is similar to and different from United States money.

Before money was invented, people used to barter, or trade. For example, Farmer John raises pigs and Farmer Katie grows carrots. Farmer John would trade a baby pig for Farmer Katie's carrots. But a pig is worth much more than a carrot, so it would take a lot of carrots to equal one pig. Even if Farmer John only needed 5 pounds of carrots, he might get 100 pounds of carrots for his pig. That is a lot of carrots to eat! And what if you had to carry a pig around every time you wanted to buy something?

▼ Before people used money, a farmer might trade to get what he or she needed.

Money Is Easy to Use

To solve the problems caused by bartering, people in Asia invented money. Instead of bartering, Farmer John could sell his pig for money. Then he could use some of the money to buy carrots and spend the rest on other things.

Money is easier in lots of ways. It can be divided into smaller amounts. Money will not fall apart, or run away! Money is easy to carry in your pocket. Using money helps make buying and selling much easier.

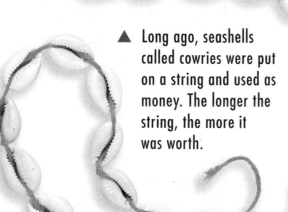

▲ Long ago, seashells called cowries were put on a string and used as money. The longer the string, the more it was worth.

QUICK CHECK

Cause and Effect **What was the effect of inventing money?**

Check Understanding

1. **VOCABULARY** Draw and label a picture to illustrate the vocabulary words below. **employee   producer   consumer**

2. **READING SKILL** Cause and Effect Use the chart from page 148 to write a paragraph about what causes prices to go up or down.

Cause	→	Effect
	→	
	→	
	→	

 3. Write About It Write a paragraph to explain how businesses in a community help people meet their needs.

155

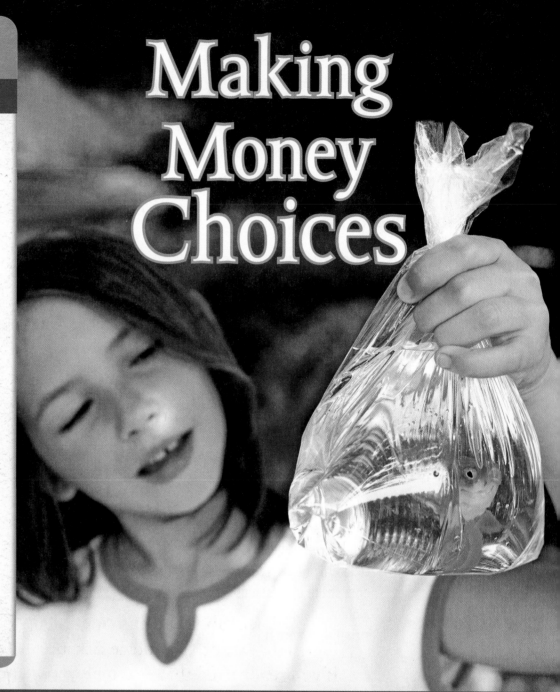

Making Money Choices

Lesson 2

VOCABULARY

budget p. 157

income p. 157

expense p. 157

opportunity cost p. 161

savings account p. 162

READING SKILL

Cause and Effect
Copy the chart below. As you read, list how a budget can help you make choices.

Cause	→	Effect
	→	
	→	
	→	

STANDARDS FOCUS

SOCIAL STUDIES Production, Distribution, and Consumption

GEOGRAPHY Human Systems

Visual Preview

How do people make choices about saving and spending money?

A People spend money on both needs and wants.

B A budget helps families plan how to spend money.

```
$15.00  (income)
-10.00  (expenses)
$ 5.00  (savings without
          popcorn)

  x 10
$50.00  (savings over
          10 weeks)
```

C A budget can help people find ways to save money.

D Some people use banks to save for what they need and want.

156

A MANAGING MONEY

Suppose you have earned enough money to buy a pet goldfish. Then you remember that you need a new tire for your bike. How do you decide how to spend your money?

People plan how to spend their money by deciding what they need and want. To help them make smart money choices, people often make a **budget**. A budget is a plan for using money.

One thing people include in a budget is **income**—the amount of money someone receives for working. An employee earns income by doing a job. A budget also includes **expenses**. An expense is something people spend money on, such as something they buy or do.

When making a budget, people first plan to pay for the things they need, like food and clothing. With the money left over, they can make choices about buying the things they want, like movie tickets. If you really need that new tire, you may have to wait to buy that pet goldfish you want!

QUICK CHECK

Cause and Effect **How does the amount of income affect what someone can buy?**

Buying a baseball mitt is an expense. Is a mitt a need or a want? ▶

B EVERYONE BUDGETS

Primary Sources

"The U.S. has never really budgeted for the kinds of unexpected things that go on every year, even though something happens every year. There's an earthquake. There's a fire. There's a hurricane."

Douglas Holtz-Eakin
Director of the Congressional Budget
Office, 2003-2005, February 6, 2006

Write About It Write a paragraph describing the kinds of expenses the United States government might have after a hurricane hits a town.

▲ Members of the United States government make decisions about the country's budget.

Not only people make budgets. Businesses make budgets, too. For example, a company that builds houses spends money on supplies, such as wood and nails. It must pay employees, too. To make sure it does not spend more money than it makes, the company includes its income and expenses in a budget.

Even the government of the United States makes a budget. Read on this page about some of the challenges the government faces in making its budget.

Family Budget

Income (per month)	Expenses	
Mom + Dad $7,800.00	Food	$250.00
	Electricity	$150.00
	Phone	$85.00
	Clothes	$500.00
	Emergencies	$1,500.00

▲ Budgets help families decide how to spend their money. Groceries are part of this family's budget.

A Family Budget

Families need budgets, too. They have to pay for things like food, electricity, and clothing. They also try to save money for the future and for emergencies—things that happen without warning. What if the car needs new brakes or the roof is leaking? A family budget should include money for emergencies such as these.

Making a budget involves decisions. It often means comparing the cost of something with the benefit of having it. A benefit is something that is good or helpful. For example, the special TV movie channel costs extra money each month. Your family loves to watch movies. The service would be a benefit, so your family has to decide if the cost is worth the benefit. If they want the special channel enough, they might even decide to give up something else to have it!

QUICK CHECK

Main Idea and Details **Why do families need to make a budget?**

C MAKING A BUDGET

Lola is 12 years old. She has a business walking her neighbors' dogs. Each week she earns an income of $15. Lola has expenses, too. Each week she goes to a movie with her friends. After the movie, she buys some treats for the dogs.

While walking the dogs one day, Lola stopped in front of a bike store. In the window, she saw the perfect bike. The price tag said $50. "I can save $50," Lola said. That night Lola made a budget. First she wrote her weekly income at the top of the budget. Then she wrote her expenses below. There was no money left over! How could Lola save money?

▼ Lola walks dogs to earn money.

My Budget $ $ $

Budget A

Income each week $15.00

Expenses each week
Bus ticket	$ 0.75
Movie ticket	4.25
Popcorn	5.00
Dog biscuits	+ 5.00
Total expenses each week	$15.00

$15.00 (income)
−15.00 (expenses)
0.00 (savings each week)

Budget B

Income each week $15.00

Total expenses each week
Bus ticket	$ 0.75
Movie ticket	4.25
Dog biscuits	+ 5.00
Total expenses without popcorn at movie	$10.00

$15.00 (income)
−10.00 (expenses)
$ 5.00 (savings without popcorn)

× 10
$50.00 (savings over 10 weeks)

Making Choices

Lola thought hard. Then she thought of a way—if she does not buy popcorn at the movies, she can save $5 a week. After ten weeks, she will have saved $50!

By choosing to save money to buy a bike, Lola also chose to stop buying a snack at the movies. This was her **opportunity cost**. An opportunity cost is the value of the thing you give up when you choose one thing instead of another. In saving for a bike, Lola's opportunity cost was not getting to eat popcorn at the movies.

QUICK CHECK

Summarize How did making a budget help Lola?

D SAVING MONEY

Money in the Bank

Lola put money into her piggy bank each week. After Lola had saved enough money for the bike, she decided to keep saving. She went to the bank and opened a **savings account**. A savings account is money a person keeps in a bank.

Lola knew her savings account would earn interest, money a bank pays people for keeping their money in the bank. The interest is added to the money Lola saves. The more money Lola saves, the more interest she earns.

Many people use banks to help them save for things they want. Benjamin Franklin, a famous American leader, knew the importance of saving. He once said,

"If you would be wealthy, think of saving as well as getting."

QUICK CHECK

Main Idea and Details **Why is it a good idea to put money into a savings account?**

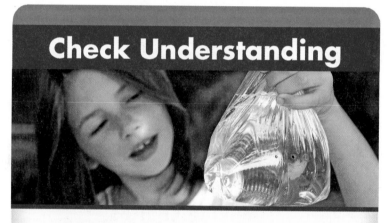

Check Understanding

1. **VOCABULARY** Write a letter to a friend about how you spent money this week. Use the following words.

   budget   income   expense

2. **READING SKILL Cause and Effect** Use your chart from page 156 to write a paragraph on how a budget can help you decide how to spend money.

Cause	→	Effect
	→	
	→	
	→	

3. **Write About It** Make a list of some ways that you could save money.

Citizenship

Points of View

How do we make decisions about spending money?

Every time we buy something we make choices. Sometimes we must give up one thing to buy something else. Read three points of view on making money choices.

Washington, D.C.

North Carolina

Missouri

"Sometimes it is better not to buy anything. Just save your money until you have enough to buy the thing you really want instead of just buying the thing you can afford right that minute."

Katie
Lee's Summit, Missouri
From an interview, 2006

"I try to budget my money. I try to make my allowance last the whole week, because something fun might come up that I might like to do that I hadn't thought of."

Jermaine
Washington, D.C.
From an interview, 2006

"You have to slow down and plan before you spend your money. I had to choose between buying a new pair of shoes or going to the movies. I picked the shoes. I knew I would get another chance to go to the movies."

Keyonna
Raleigh, North Carolina
From an interview, 2006

Write About It Write a paragraph about choosing to buy one thing over another.

Farm Communities

VOCABULARY

human resource p. 165

capital resource p. 165

demand p. 168

supply p. 168

scarcity p. 168

READING SKILL

Cause and Effect
Copy the chart below. As you read, list the ways that supply affects price.

Cause	→	Effect
	→	
	→	
	→	

STANDARDS FOCUS

SOCIAL STUDIES · Production, Distribution, and Consumption

GEOGRAPHY · Environment and Society

Wheat is an important farm product.

Visual Preview

How do farmers produce goods for the economy?

A Farmers use many resources to grow crops.

B Different crops grow in different regions of the country.

C The price of a crop depends on how much of it there is.

THE BUSINESS OF FARMING

Beautiful, golden grains of wheat! Somewhere a farmer worked hard to grow the wheat to make your bread, rolls, and muffins.

Agriculture is an important part of the United States economy. Agriculture is the business of growing crops or raising animals for food. From apples to corn to wheat to zucchini, a lot of work is involved in getting the food we buy to market.

Farmers use natural resources—soil, water, and sunlight—to grow crops. They also need **human resources**, the people, both employers and employees, who work for a business. **Capital resources** are needed, too. Capital resources are the tools, machines, and buildings people use to produce goods.

Tractors and computers are some capital resources farmers use. Stores sell farmers the resources and supplies they need. Farmers sometimes borrow money from banks to buy capital resources. They make an agreement with the banks to pay the money back.

QUICK CHECK

Cause and Effect Why do farmers sometimes borrow money from banks?

This tractor is a capital resource. ▶

165

FARMS AND PRODUCTS

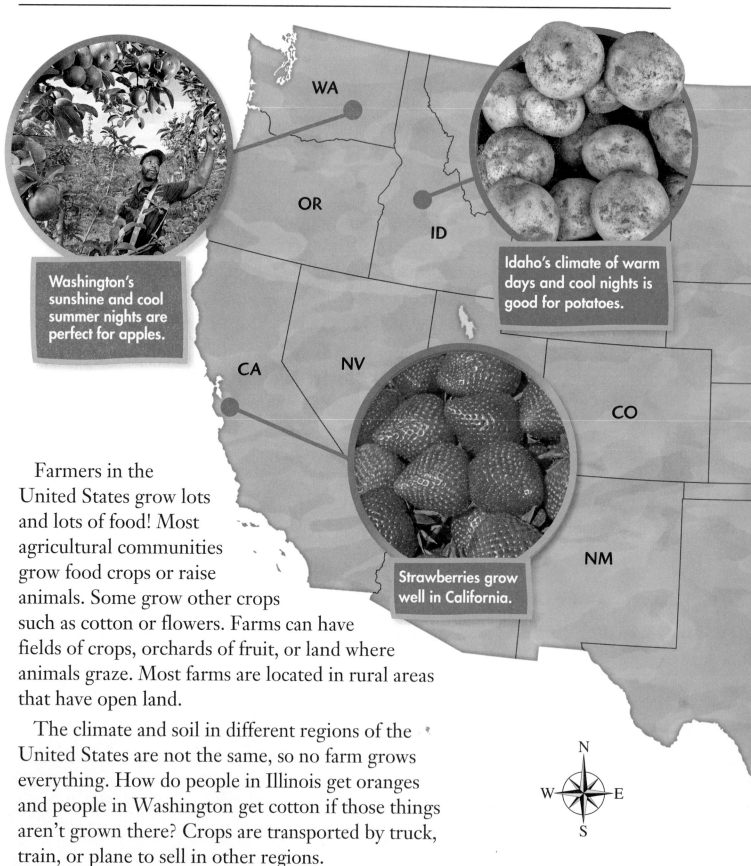

Washington's sunshine and cool summer nights are perfect for apples.

Idaho's climate of warm days and cool nights is good for potatoes.

Strawberries grow well in California.

WA

OR

ID

CA

NV

CO

NM

N
W   E
S

Farmers in the United States grow lots and lots of food! Most agricultural communities grow food crops or raise animals. Some grow other crops such as cotton or flowers. Farms can have fields of crops, orchards of fruit, or land where animals graze. Most farms are located in rural areas that have open land.

The climate and soil in different regions of the United States are not the same, so no farm grows everything. How do people in Illinois get oranges and people in Washington get cotton if those things aren't grown there? Crops are transported by truck, train, or plane to sell in other regions.

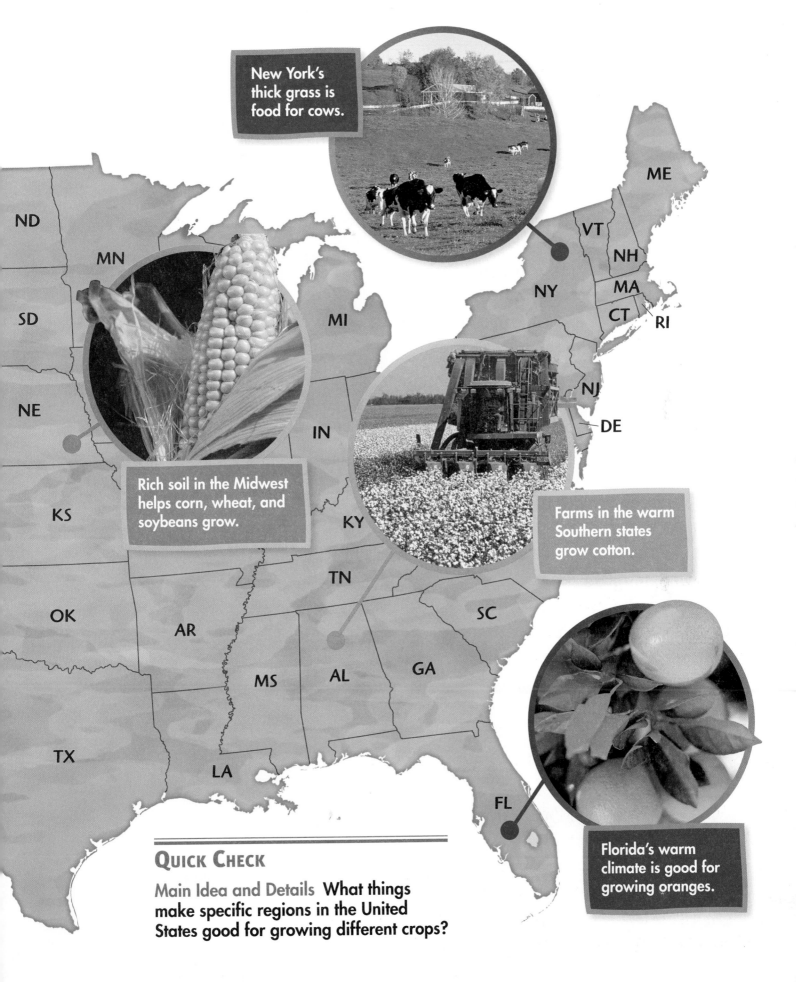

New York's thick grass is food for cows.

ME

VT

NH

MA

CT

RI

NY

NJ

DE

ND

MN

SD

MI

NE

IN

Rich soil in the Midwest helps corn, wheat, and soybeans grow.

KS

KY

TN

Farms in the warm Southern states grow cotton.

OK

AR

SC

AL

GA

MS

TX

LA

FL

Florida's warm climate is good for growing oranges.

QUICK CHECK

Main Idea and Details What things make specific regions in the United States good for growing different crops?

167

Everyone needs to eat, so there is always a high **demand** for food. Demand is the number of people who want certain goods or services.

Suppose corn is for sale at a farmers' market. If only one farmer is selling corn, there is a low **supply**. Supply is the amount of goods or services that are available. A small supply of corn leads to **scarcity**. Scarcity means a shortage of certain goods or services.

If lots of people want to buy corn, then there is a high demand. As people line up to buy the corn, the farmer may raise the price. Since the demand is high and only one farmer is selling it, many people are willing to pay the higher price.

High demand means the farmer can charge more for his corn. ▶

EVENT

Each year there is an art and pumpkin festival held in Half Moon Bay, California. On display at the festival is the winner of the **Great Pumpkin Weigh-Off**. The largest pumpkin in 2006 was 1,223 pounds!

Great Pumpkin Weigh-Off

Making Choices

What if the demand for corn is high, but there is a scarcity of human resources to pick the corn? A farm owner might have employees who usually do other jobs pick corn instead. Then the farmer will have enough corn to meet the high demand. When human resources or capital resources are low, farm owners need to make choices about how they use their resources.

Some people might not pay the high price for the corn. They may go to a grocery store to look for cheaper corn, or even buy something else. This is how our free enterprise economy works. Free enterprise is the freedom to run your business the way you decide. It is also the freedom to buy from whomever you want.

▲ Grocery stores buy a lot of corn, so they often sell it at lower prices.

QUICK CHECK

Summarize **What is a free enterprise economy?**

Check Understanding

1. **VOCABULARY** Write a sentence to explain each vocabulary term below.
   human resource   **capital resource**
   supply   **scarcity**

2. **READING SKILLS Cause and Effect** Use your chart from page 164 to write a paragraph about how supply affects price.

3. **Write About It** W
   explaining why you d
   something at a cer

Chart and Graph Skills

Use Line Graphs

VOCABULARY

line graph

Suppose you are reading a book about farms in the United States. You come to a diagram like the one below. It is a **line graph**. A line graph shows information that changes over time. Let's see how to get information from a line graph.

Learn It

- Read the title. The graph title tells you that this graph is about farms in the United States from 1950 to 2000.

- The numbers on the left show the number of farms. The years are shown at the bottom.

- To read the graph, find the dot above each year. Put your finger on the dot, then move it to the left to find the number of farms for that year.

- The dots are connected to make a line. The line shows that the number of farms has gone down since 1950.

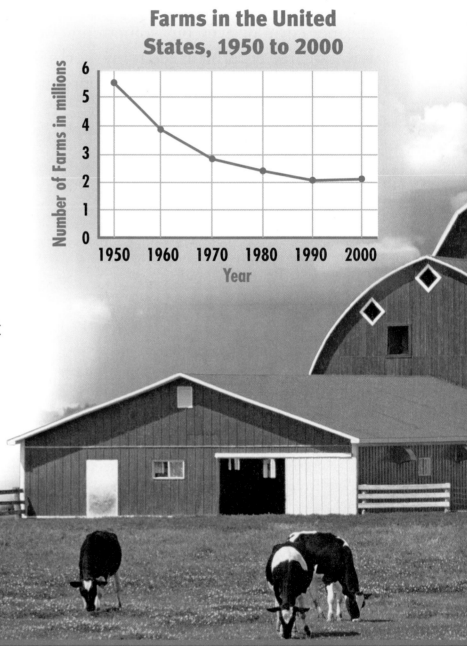

Farms in the United States, 1950 to 2000

Number of Farms in millions

Year

Try It

Look at the graph at right.

● What does this graph show?

● What do the numbers on the left show?

● How did the amount of land used for farming change between 1950 and 2000?

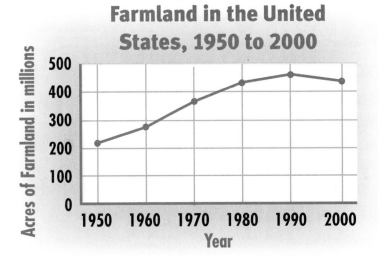

Farmland in the United States, 1950 to 2000

Acres of Farmland in millions

500
400
300
200
100
0

1950 1960 1970 1980 1990 2000

Year

Apply It

Now make your own line graph. Use this information about a third-grade class that printed and sold T-shirts.

Week 1, 10 T-shirts sold
Week 2, 20 T-shirts sold
Week 3, 50 T-shirts sold
Week 4, 25 T-shirts sold

● What title will you give your graph?

● What information will you put at the bottom of the graph? What will you put along the side?

● What does the graph tell you about the class's T-shirt sale?

Making Goods

VOCABULARY

factory p. 173

specialize p. 176

import p. 178

export p. 179

READING SKILL

Cause and Effect
Copy the chart below. As you read, list ways the growth of the auto industry affected other industries.

Cause	→	Effect
	→	
	→	
	→	

STANDARDS FOCUS

SOCIAL STUDIES — Production, Distribution, and Consumption

GEOGRAPHY — Environment and Society

Workers follow many steps to manufacture airplanes.

Visual Preview

How do communities meet their needs for goods?

A New methods helped produce goods quickly and more cheaply.

B Many factories and towns were built to produce manufactured goods.

C People can buy products that are made in other nations.

D The United States trades with other nations to get the products it needs.

A A FASTER WAY

As the line of cars moves along, workers and machines put them together. Your job is to put the doors on. When the car reaches the end of the line, it is complete.

In 1885 the first automobile was built in Europe. By 1900 companies in the United States had started manufacturing autos, too. Manufacturing, or the making of goods by machines, is an important part of the United States economy. A place where goods are manufactured is called a **factory**.

In 1903 Henry Ford started the Ford Motor Company in Detroit, Michigan. At first each car was built from start to finish by one or two people. Each car took a long time to build, so cars were very expensive. By 1913 Ford began using assembly lines in his factories. On an assembly line, each worker has a specific job to do, like putting on wheels or windows. Building cars this way is much faster and costs less money.

QUICK CHECK

Cause and Effect **How did Henry Ford change car manufacturing?**

Factories today still use assembly lines to manufacture many products. ▶

In the late 1880s, steel factories were built in Pittsburgh, Pennsylvania; Gary, Indiana; and Chicago, Illinois, because these places were near coal mining areas.

Many people came to work in the steel mills. The towns around the mills grew rapidly.

B GROWTH OF MANUFACTURING

As the price of cars came down, many more people could afford one. That meant the demand for cars went up, so manufacturers opened more factories and hired more employees to meet the demand. Automobile manufacturing became a huge part of the United States economy.

Today steel is made in new, less expensive ways. One new way uses scrap steel recycled from old bridges, refrigerators, and cars.

Steel manufacturing has made it possible for the United States to make many goods, including machines, tools, bridges, and railroad tracks.

Steel Manufacturing

To make cars, factories needed steel. Lots of steel! That meant the steel industry grew, too. Making steel uses both iron ore and coal, so steel factories were built near where these natural resources were found. The United States still makes many kinds of steel for many different steel products, from playground equipment to pots and pans.

QUICK CHECK

Cause and Effect **What made the steel industry grow?**

A WORLD OF PRODUCTS

Some businesses or regions make certain products better than others. When businesses or regions have people who are good at making something, they can **specialize** in that product. To specialize means to make one thing very well. Perhaps a region is located near natural resources that are needed to make something. The businesses there can specialize in certain products because they have the resources they need to make them.

Specialized Products

In the 1940s, the United States specialized in making steel and steel products. Why? It was because the United States had plenty of iron ore and coal. Pittsburgh, Gary, and Chicago became known as "steel towns."

Other countries specialize, too. Spain and Greece specialize in producing olive oil. Switzerland is famous for making watches. Japan is known for electronics. China produces many types of clothing. These countries have what they need to make these products faster, better, or at a lower cost.

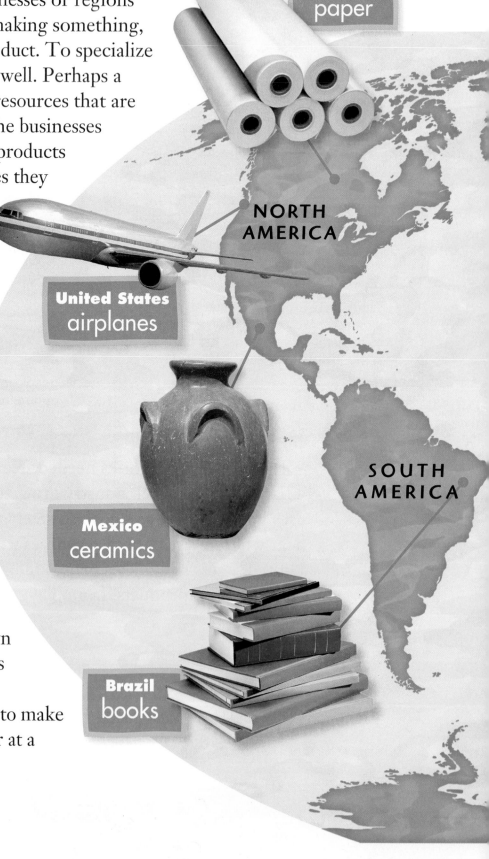

Canada
paper

NORTH
AMERICA

United States
airplanes

Mexico
ceramics

SOUTH
AMERICA

Brazil
books

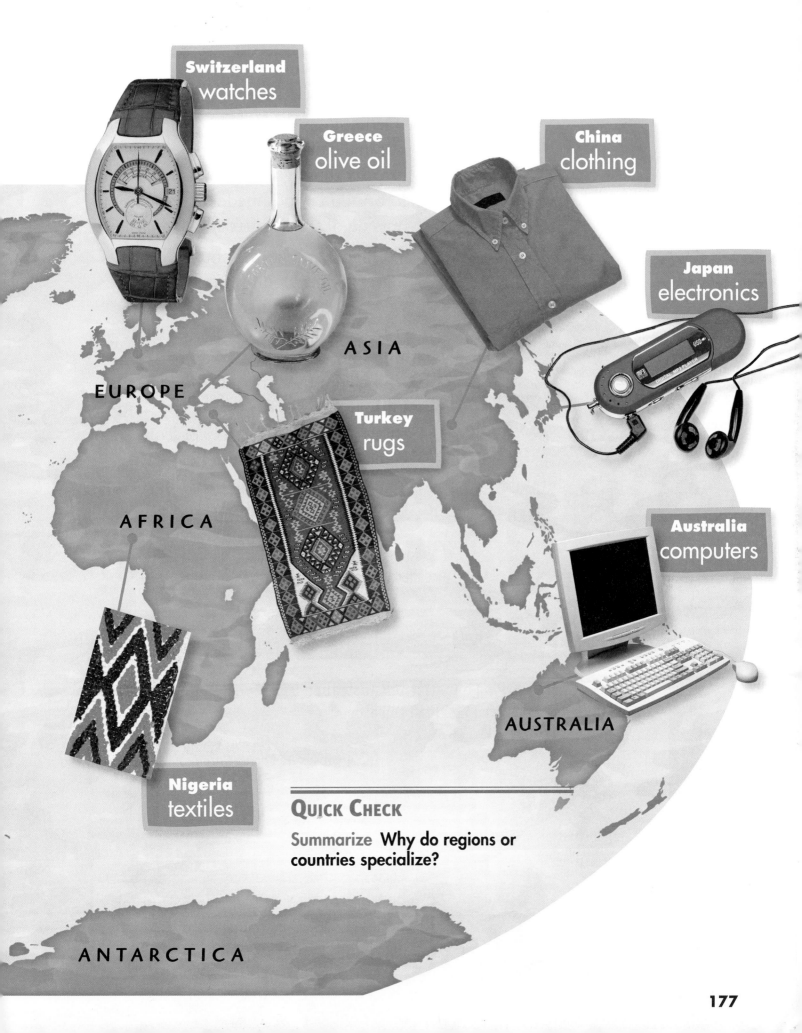

Switzerland watches

Greece olive oil

China clothing

Japan electronics

Turkey rugs

Australia computers

Nigeria textiles

EUROPE

ASIA

AFRICA

AUSTRALIA

ANTARCTICA

QUICK CHECK

Summarize **Why do regions or countries specialize?**

D GOODS IN AND OUT

What does a country do when it does not make or grow something? It will **import** those goods. To import means to bring in goods made or grown outside of the country for sale or use.

The climate in most of the United States is not good for growing coffee beans. So the United States imports coffee beans from Central America and South America. It imports many fruits from these places, too. The United States also imports toys and shoes from China, and beef from Canada. Read the quote below to learn about some other products that the United States imports.

◀ Most of the bananas sold in the United States are imported.

Primary Sources

"Americans are growing hungrier for Australian beef, Canadian pork, Chilean plums, and Mexican tomatoes."

A quote from
the *Arkansas Democrat-Gazette*,
April 16, 2006

Write About It Write a paragraph about why you think Americans are "growing hungrier" for these products.

▲ Large ships carry imports and exports all over the world.

When a country makes a lot of something, it can **export** that product. To export means to send goods out of a country to be sold somewhere else. The United States exports many things, such as cars to Canada and wheat to Japan. Importing and exporting helps the economies of both countries.

QUICK CHECK

Main Idea and Details **What can a country do to get products that it does not produce?**

Check Understanding

1. **VOCABULARY** Use the words below to write a paragraph about making goods.
   factory   specialize   export

2. **READING SKILL Cause and Effect** Use your chart from page 172 to write a paragraph about how the growth of the auto industry affected other industries.

Cause	→	Effect
	→	
	→	
	→	

 3. **Write About It** Write a paragraph to explain why countries import goods.

Lesson 5

VOCABULARY

international trade p. 182

domestic trade p. 184

cooperate p. 186

READING SKILL

Cause and Effect
Copy the chart below. As you read, list ways communities work together.

Cause	→	Effect
	→	
	→	
	→	

STANDARDS FOCUS

SOCIAL STUDIES Global Connections

GEOGRAPHY Human Systems

WORKING TOGETHER

Working on the International Space Station

Visual Preview

How do communities work together?

A People from many countries help each other.

B Countries all over the world buy and sell goods to one another.

C People in different states work together to make goods like this book.

D Cities in the United States form ties with cities in other countries.

COUNTRIES WORK TOGETHER

It is November 2000. You are aboard the space shuttle with United States astronauts and Russian cosmonauts. There is much work to do, and everyone must work together!

Countries often work together so they can learn from one another. The United States, Russia, and other countries shared ideas to build the International Space Station. Astronauts from different countries continue to live and work at the space station today. They do experiments and research to help improve life on Earth and to search for possible life on other planets.

Countries also work together on Earth to help those in need. Some doctors and nurses work for an international group called Doctors Without Borders. They travel around the world to care for sick people. Groups like this one, which started in France, work to improve hospitals and health services in many countries.

QUICK CHECK

Cause and Effect **What are some reasons countries sometimes work together?**

A doctor gives a baby a health checkup. ▶

181

B TRADING TOGETHER

Another way countries work together is to exchange goods. What if there are goods that the United States needs that are not made or grown here? Then the United States trades with other countries to get what it needs. Trade between different countries is called **international trade**. For example, the United States exports cars to Canada and imports Canadian wood.

Countries import goods they need and export goods they specialize in making. Trading with each other helps the economies of both countries.

Saudi Arabia, a country in the Middle East, does not make cars. It buys them from other countries, including the United States. The United States needs more oil than it can produce, so it imports oil from Saudi Arabia.

PEOPLE

Vivienne Tam is a clothing designer in New York City. She also works with young designers in Hong Kong and China, her home country. People all over the world wear Vivienne Tam's clothing.

Vivienne Tam

The United States exports cars to many other countries. The United States also imports cars that other countries make. You can see information about this international car trade in the Datagraphic below.

QUICK CHECK

Summarize How does trading together help both countries?

DataGraphic
Trading Partners

The United States does a lot of business in cars! The graph and map show you the major countries for this car exchange.

U.S. Car Imports, 2005

Canada	🚗🚗🚗🚗🚗🚗🚗🚗🚗🚗🚗🚗🚗🚗
Germany	🚗🚗🚗🚗🚗🚗🚗🚗🚗🚗🚗
Japan	🚗🚗🚗🚗🚗🚗🚗🚗🚗🚗🚗🚗🚗🚗🚗🚗🚗🚗🚗

🚗 = $2 billion in car sales

U.S. Car Exports, 2005

🚗 = $2 billion

Source: Bureau of Economic Analysis, U.S. Department of Commerce, 2006

Think About Imports and Exports

1. How many billions of dollars worth of cars does the United States import from Germany?

2. With which country does the United States both buy and sell cars?

Most states in the United States specialize in making something. States are proud of their products and may put labels on them, like Florida oranges or Washington apples.

States also trade their goods and services. Wherever you live, you can buy goods made in other states. This is **domestic trade**. Unlike international trade, domestic trade is trade that takes place within the borders of a country.

New York City, New York

1 The pages of your textbook are written in New York City, New York. Once the writing and corrections are done, the pages are sent to be printed.

Willard, Ohio

2 In Willard, Ohio, the pages of your textbook are printed and bound together to make a book. Thousands of textbooks are printed here.

People in several states worked together to produce your textbook. It was written in one state and printed in another. The paper it was printed on came from still another state. Look at the map and boxes on these pages to see how people in different states worked together to make your textbook and get it to classrooms like yours.

DeSoto, Texas

3 The finished textbooks are shipped to a warehouse in DeSoto, Texas. A warehouse is a building where goods are stored until they are sold.

QUICK CHECK

Summarize **How is domestic trade different from international trade?**

Chicago's Sister Cities

Chicago, United States

Mexico City, Mexico

Map Skill

LOCATION Which of Chicago's sister cities are shown on the map?

Ⓓ SISTER CITIES

In 1956 President Dwight D. Eisenhower set up a program so that cities in the United States could form partnerships with "sister" cities in other countries. People in sister cities agree to learn about culture, trade, and government in each other's community.

The people of sister cities **cooperate** with each other. To cooperate means to work together. Sister cities cooperate by helping people in need, opening new businesses, and sharing their cultures. Chicago, Illinois, has 21 sister cities all over the world. The people of Chicago learn about different cultures by sharing with people in their sister cities.

EVENT

The yearly **North Carolina International Festival** is held in Raleigh. At this event, the community celebrates world cultures through art, storytelling, food, and dance.

North Carolina International Festival

Galway, Ireland

Moscow, Russia

Paris, France

Osaka, Japan

Durban, South Africa

Traveling and Learning

Students from Lake View High School in Chicago traveled to Paris, France—one of their sister cities. They had a wonderful time talking with French students and seeing sights like the Eiffel Tower. Yury G., one of the Chicago students, said,

" They were so nice and friendly to us. Even though sometimes we couldn't find the right word in English or French, we managed to communicate. **"**

QUICK CHECK

Main Idea and Details **How do sister cities cooperate?**

Check Understanding

1. **VOCABULARY** Write a sentence for each of the vocabulary words below.
   international trade   domestic trade   cooperate

2. **READING SKILL Cause and Effect** Use your chart from page 180 to write a paragraph about ways communities work together.

Cause	→	Effect
	→	
	→	
	→	

3. **Write About It** Write a paragraph telling how communities benefit from having sister cities.

Local Connections

Businesses in Your Community

Peter lives in Carlinville, Illinois. He learned about businesses in his community by interviewing people. When Peter got home, he made an accordion book about what he found out. Here's what you can do to learn about businesses in your community:

- Make a list of businesses or jobs in your community that interest you.

- Think of questions you would like to ask people about working in those businesses.

- Have an adult come with you to interview people at three different businesses. Bring a pencil and notebook. Write down what each worker tells you. If you have a camera, ask if you can take pictures of them at work.

For more help with your project visit
www.macmillanmh.com

Economics Activity

Make an Accordion Book

1 Gather the notes and photos you took during the interviews.

2 To make your book, start with a large piece of stiff paper. Paper that is 36" long by 8" wide is a good size. Fold the paper into even parts.

3 On each page, write the name of a worker you interviewed and paste a photo of the person. Summarize the things the worker told you, and write them below the photo or on the back. Make a cover for your book, and give your book a title.

4 Share your book with your classmates.

Materials
- notebook
- pencil or pen
- camera
- poster board
- markers
- scissors
- glue

1. Construction Worker
2. Librarian
3. Banker
4. Shop Owner
5. Police person

Unit 4 Review and Assess

Vocabulary

Write a sentence or more to answer each question.

1. If you ran a business, how could you be sure you made a **profit**?

2. What are examples of **expenses** a family has?

3. Which do you think are more important in running a business, **human resources** or **capital resources**?

4. Find something in your home that was **imported** from another country and tell where it is from.

Comprehension and Critical Thinking

5. How does a business figure out if it made a profit?

6. How does the United States get the goods it needs?

7. **Critical Thinking** What kinds of things would you include in a family budget?

8. **Reading Skill** What usually happens to the price of something when there is a scarcity of that thing?

Skill

Use Line Graphs

Write a complete sentence to answer each question.

9. What was the population of the United States in 1970?

10. Did the United States have more people or fewer people in 2000 than it did in 1970?

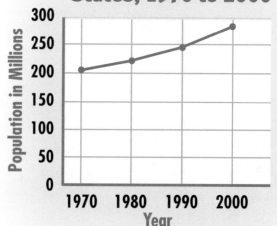

Population of the United States, 1970 to 2000

 # Test Preparation

Look at the chart. Then answer the questions.

Top United States Exports and Imports in 2006

Export	Import
1. machines (airplanes, computers, cars)	1. machines (cars, telephones)
2. scientific tools	2. clothes, shoes, toys
3. chemicals, plastic	3. iron, steel, paper
4. metal, paper	4. oil
5. crops and animals	5. chemicals

1. The United States imports

   A. crops and oil.

   B. scientific tools.

   C. metal and paper.

   D. oil and chemicals.

2. Which of the following items does the United States send to other countries to be sold?

   A. telephones

   B. toys

   C. shoes

   D. airplanes

3. Which of the following items does the United States both import and export?

   A. oil

   B. chemicals

   C. crops and animals

   D. scientific tools

4. Why do you think the United States both imports and exports cars?

5. Name something you use every day that was imported from another country.

The Big Idea Activities

How do people in a community meet their needs?

Write About the Big Idea

Expository Composition

Think about what you learned in Unit 4 about the ways people meet their needs. Use the notes you made on your foldable to write an essay to answer the Big Idea question. Be sure to begin with a sentence that tells the topic of the composition. Include one paragraph for each way that people meet their needs. Include causes and effects, and give examples from your own community. End with a concluding paragraph.

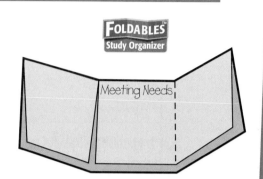

Meeting Needs

Projects About the Big Idea

Make a Budget Suppose you are starting a lemonade business. Make a budget that shows your expenses and your income. Include in your budget the costs of different ways of making lemonade. Then decide which way would be the best for your business.

Make a Poster You just heard that a new, bigger baseball park is being built in your community. How will this change your community and its economy? What will the new park replace? Make a poster showing why you think the decision to build this baseball park is good or bad for the community.

Income per week:		Cost of lemons and sugar:	
sell 1 cup of lemonade	$1.00	12 lemons	$2.00
sell 15 cups in 1 week	$15.00	1 box sugar	$1.00
Expenses per week:		Cost of lemonade mix:	
cups	$3.00	Brand A	$4.00
lemons and sugar	$3.00	Brand B	$5.00

lemonade from lemons and sugar?
Use lemonade mix and lemons?
Brand B mix costs more but it tastes better than Brand A—is it worth it?

192 Unit 4

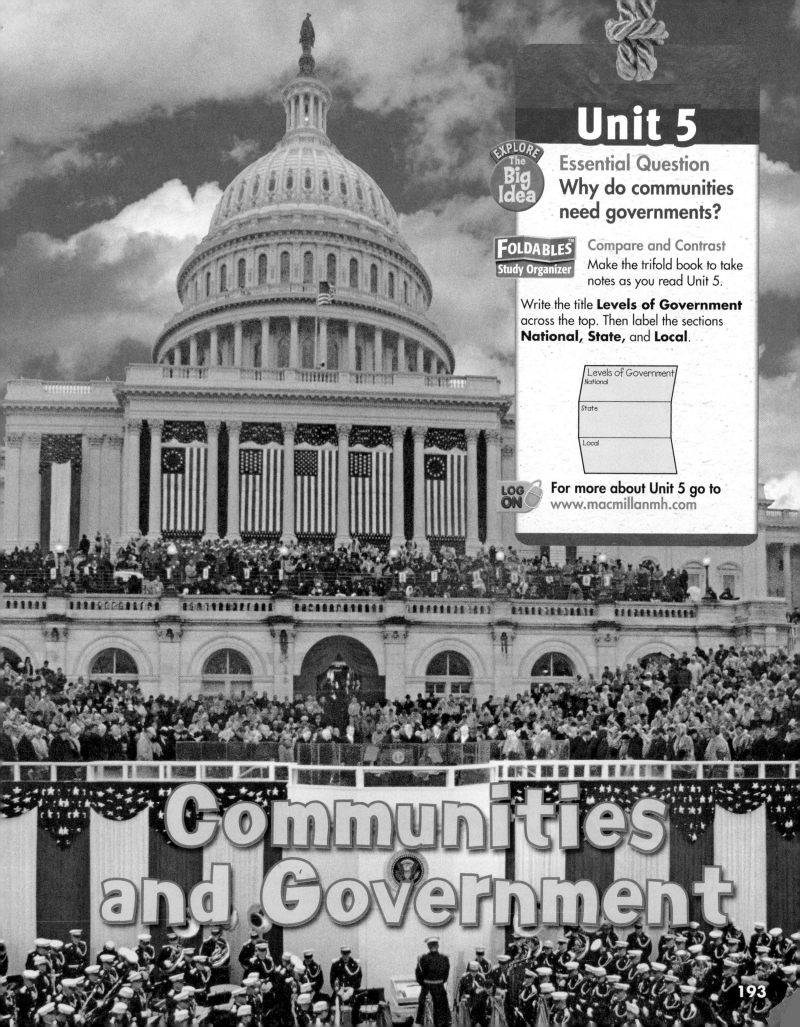

Unit 5

EXPLORE The Big Idea

Essential Question
Why do communities need governments?

FOLDABLES™ Study Organizer

Compare and Contrast
Make the trifold book to take notes as you read Unit 5.

Write the title **Levels of Government** across the top. Then label the sections **National, State,** and **Local.**

Levels of Government
National

State

Local

LOG ON **For more about Unit 5 go to**
www.macmillanmh.com

Communities and Government

193

PEOPLE, PLACES, AND EVENTS

Elizabeth Cady Stanton and Lucretia Mott

Seneca Falls, New York

Seneca Falls Convention

1848
Men and women meet to discuss women's rights at the Seneca Falls Convention.

Elizabeth Cady Stanton and **Lucretia Mott** spoke at the **Seneca Falls Convention** about the importance of women's rights, including the right to vote.

Today you can visit the site where this meeting took place.

Students at Wells Memorial
School, Harrisville, NH

New Hampshire

New Hampshire state fruit

2006 Pumpkin proclaimed state fruit by New
Hampshire Legislature.

Third- and fourth-grade students worked with government
leaders to make the pumpkin **New Hampshire's** state fruit.

Today young people can work with their government to help
their state or community.

National Government

Lesson 1

VOCABULARY

citizen p. 197

executive branch p. 198

legislative branch p. 199

judicial branch p. 199

READING SKILL

Compare and Contrast
Copy the diagram below. As you read, use the diagram to show how two branches of government are alike and different.

Different Alike Different

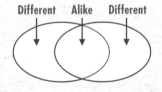

STANDARDS FOCUS

SOCIAL STUDIES   Civic Ideals and Practices

GEOGRAPHY   Human Systems

Visual Preview

What is important to know about our national government?

A The United States government protects the rights of citizens.

B The national government has three branches that share power.

C "The Star-Spangled Banner" is a symbol of our country.

D America has other symbols that stand for our country's values.

196

PROTECTING RIGHTS

Does your class have a list of classroom rules? Why do you think there are rules? What would you do if you thought a classroom rule was unfair?

Why do countries have governments? The United States government works to protect the rights of its **citizens**. A citizen is a person who lives in a community and has certain rights and responsibilities, or duties. Our government makes laws to protect our rights, to be sure all people are treated fairly, and to keep us safe.

All citizens have the right to gather peacefully. ▼

American Freedoms

The United States Constitution is our most important law. The Constitution protects our five basic rights, or freedoms. They are the freedom to practice any religion, the freedom to meet peacefully in groups, the freedom to say what we think, the freedom to write what we think, and the right to ask the government for help if we think we are treated unfairly. All the laws our government makes must protect these rights. In return, citizens are asked to take part in government by voting in elections and by paying taxes.

QUICK CHECK

Compare and Contrast How are rights different from responsibilities?

197

The leaders who wrote the Constitution did not want any one part of the government to have all the power. So they divided the government into three parts, or branches. Each branch has a job to do. Each branch works in its own building in our nation's capital, Washington, D.C.

The White House

The President is the head of the executive branch, the part of government that carries out laws. The executive branch cannot make the laws, but the President must say yes or no to each new law that Congress makes. This power to say no to a law is called a veto.

Library of Congress

Lincoln Memorial

Washington Monument

The Capitol

The legislative branch, called Congress, is the part of government that writes laws. This branch has two parts—the House of Representatives and the Senate. Members of the two parts come from all 50 states. To pass a law, both parts must agree.

The Supreme Court

Sometimes laws that are passed may not be fair. The judicial branch decides if laws are fair and follow the Constitution. This branch is made up of our courts and judges. The Supreme Court, with nine judges, is the country's most powerful court.

Natural History Museum

National Gallery of Art

Smithsonian Castle

Air and Space Museum

QUICK CHECK

Compare and Contrast What are the jobs of each branch of government?

199

C   A SONG ABOUT FREEDOM

"The Star-Spangled Banner" is America's national anthem, or official song, and a well-known symbol of our country. You can read the words and music to "The Star-Spangled Banner" on the next page.

The Song Tells a Story

In 1814 the United States was fighting a war against the British. One rainy night, a man named Francis Scott Key watched British ships firing on an American fort. An American flag flew over the fort, but soon it got too dark for Key to see the flag.

Key knew that if the British captured the fort, they would take down the American flag. In the morning Key saw that the flag was still there! He knew then that the Americans had won the battle.

Key wrote a poem about what he had seen. In time people began to sing the poem to the tune of an old British song. In 1931, more than 100 years later, the song became our national anthem.

QUICK CHECK

Summarize What was Key describing when he wrote "The Star-Spangled Banner"?

The Star-Spangled Banner

Music Attributed to J.S. Smith
Words by Francis Scott Key

Oh,___ say, can you see, by the dawn's ear - ly light,

What so proud - ly we hailed at the twi-light's last gleam-ing?

Whose broad stripes and bright stars, through the per - il - ous fight,

O'er the ram - parts we watched were so gal - lant - ly stream-ing?

And the rock - ets' red glare, the bombs burst-ing in air,

Gave proof through the night that our flag was still there.

Oh, say, does that___ Star-Span-gled Ban - ner___ yet wave___

O'er the land___ of the free and the home of the brave?

D AMERICAN SYMBOLS

As you've just read, "The Star-Spangled Banner" is an important symbol of our country. Another important symbol is the flag itself. The United States flag reminds us of the freedom and values we share as Americans. We display it on national holidays and on many other special occasions. Americans show respect for the flag and the ideas it represents by reciting the Pledge of Allegiance. Read the Pledge below.

Primary Sources

"I pledge allegiance [loyalty] to the flag of the United States of America, and to the Republic [government] for which it stands, one Nation under God, indivisible [not divided], with liberty and justice for all."

First written by Francis Bellamy, 1892

Write About It Which words of the Pledge of Allegiance describe rights people have?

▼ Many students begin the school day by saying the Pledge of Allegiance.

▲ The bald eagle, our national bird, is another symbol of our country.

▲ The words on the bell say, "Proclaim Liberty throughout all the Land. . . ."

The Liberty Bell

The Liberty Bell has rung for many important events. Its most famous ringing was on July 8, 1776, when it called citizens of Philadelphia to hear the reading of the Declaration of Independence. Later, in 1837, a group that worked to end slavery used the bell as a symbol of liberty.

Because it is cracked, the Liberty Bell can no longer be rung. But each year on the Fourth of July it is gently tapped 13 times by descendants of the Declaration's signers.

QUICK CHECK

Summarize **What do many American symbols represent?**

Check Understanding

1. **VOCABULARY** Write a sentence to explain each term below.
   executive branch   **judicial branch**
   legislative branch

2. **READING SKILL** Compare and Contrast Use your diagram from page 196 to write a paragraph about how two branches of national government are alike and different.

3. **Write About It** Write a letter to tell a friend something important you learned about our national government.

Chart and Graph Skills

Use Flow Charts

VOCABULARY

flow chart

Suppose your class decides to elect a class president. There are several steps to follow. These steps have to be done in a certain order. A **flow chart** shows the different steps to complete a process. A flow chart can help you understand and remember the steps in the right order.

Learn It

Look at the chart as you read.

- **Read the title.** This flow chart shows the steps for electing a class president.

- **Look at the pictures and read the captions.** Both pictures and captions give information.

- **The arrows and numbers show the order of the steps.** Start at the top and follow the arrows. The steps are done in order. Flow charts are read from top to bottom, like this one, or from left to right.

Electing a Class President

Students tell why they should be chosen class president.

Students vote for the person they think will do the best job.

Someone fair counts the votes.

The student with the most votes becomes the class president.

Try It

Now read the flow chart on this page and answer the questions.

- What does the chart show?

- What is the first step? What is the last step?

- What happens just before the President signs the bill?

- Does Congress vote on the bill before or after the President signs it?

Apply It

Do you know how to make a sandwich, plant a garden, or make papier-mâché?

Make your own flow chart to show the steps. Make a list of steps. Tell them in order. Draw a picture to show each step. Use arrows and numbers to show the order of the steps. Give your chart a title.

Share your flow chart with your classmates.

An Idea Becomes a Law

People get an idea for a new law.

A representative presents the idea to Congress. The idea is called a bill.

Congress votes "yes" on the bill.

The president signs the bill into law.

Lesson 2

State Government

VOCABULARY

governor p. 207

capitol p. 207

READING SKILL

Compare and Contrast
Copy the diagram below. As you read, use it to show how state and national governments are alike and different.

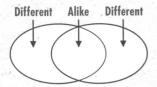

Different   Alike   Different

STANDARDS FOCUS

SOCIAL STUDIES Power, Authority, and Governance

SOCIAL STUDIES Human Systems

◄ Governor Janet Napolitano of Arizona

Visual Preview

How do state governments help the community?

A Our state governments have three branches that share power.

B States use tax money to pay for services such as schools and highways.

C States provide services such as law enforcement and parks.

Did you know that each state has its own government?
How is state government like national government?
Let's look at state government in Arizona.

Like our national government, state governments are divided into three branches. A **governor** is a person elected to be head of a state's executive branch. In 2006 the citizens of Arizona reelected Janet Napolitano to be their governor. Governor Napolitano helps carry out Arizona's laws.

Arizona has a legislative branch, too. Members of the legislative branch write laws. The judges in Arizona's judicial branch make sure state laws agree with Arizona's constitution. All three branches of Arizona government work in Phoenix, the state capital. As in national government, all branches of Arizona government work together for the people in their state.

PLACES

This building was once the Arizona state capitol. A **capitol** is a building in which the state or national government meets. Today the building is a museum. Members of Arizona government now work in buildings near the **Arizona State Capitol Museum**.

Arizona State Capitol Museum

QUICK CHECK

Compare and Contrast **How is the executive branch of a state government like the executive branch of national government?**

State government provides services, such as schools, parks, and highways. All these things cost money! Did you ever wonder how the government pays for these services? It uses tax money collected from its citizens.

People pay sales tax on things they buy. ▼

▲ State taxes help pay for schools and colleges.

Different Kinds of Taxes

There are many kinds of taxes. Some are federal, or national, taxes. People who work pay income tax to the federal government. Many states have an income tax, too. Some states, like Arizona, also have a sales tax. That means people pay a little extra on some things they buy. A price tag on a shirt says $14.00, but you might pay $14.79. The extra 79 cents is the sales tax. This money goes to the state government.

Taxes in Arizona

Citizens of Arizona pay taxes to their state government. The taxes help pay for government services. The graphs below show how Arizona spent its tax money.

DataGraphic
Arizona Tax Money

Study the two graphs. Then answer the questions.

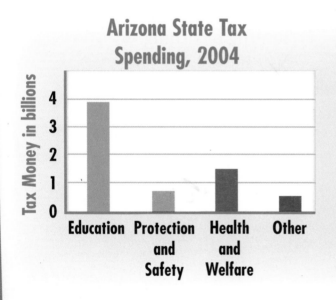

Arizona State Tax Spending, 2004

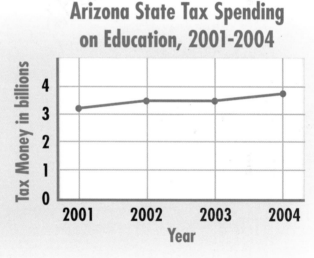

Arizona State Tax Spending on Education, 2001-2004

Source: *Arizona Office of Finance and Budgeting, 2006*

Think About Arizona Tax Dollars

1. Which item got the most of Arizona's tax money in 2004?

2. Did the amount of money spent on education in Arizona go up or down from 2001 to 2004?

QUICK CHECK

Summarize **What are some things that tax money is used for?**

State governments provide many services. States build and take care of state highways. States run health programs, and build colleges. State governments also give money to help local schools.

States make license plates for cars and trucks. States issue licenses to people, too. A license shows that you have the skill to do something, such as drive a car, or that you have permission for an activity, such as hunting or fishing.

▲ Doctors must have a license from their state government to take care of people.

State governments hire police officers to keep state highways safe. ▼

▲ Kartchner Caverns State Park opened in 1999. The men who found the cave kept it a secret until they were sure it would be protected.

Protecting the Environment

State governments also work to protect the environment. States set aside land to keep plants, animals, and other natural resources safe. In 1974, two men discovered an unique cave with unusual colors and rock formation in the mountains near Benson, Arizona. The state government bought the cave and the land around it to protect it. The area is now Kartchner Caverns State Park.

QUICK CHECK

Summarize **What are some services that state governments provide?**

Check Understanding

1. **VOCABULARY** Research your state's governor. Then write a sentence about him or her using the following words.
   governor   **capitol**

2. **READING SKILL**
   Compare and Contrast
   Use your diagram from page 206 to write a paragraph about how state and national governments are alike and different.

3. **Write About It** Write a letter to your state's governor. Give your opinion about something you think is important in your state.

Map and Globe Skills

Use Road Maps

VOCABULARY

road map

interstate
  highway

state highway

Suppose you and your family are driving in Indiana. How would you know which roads to take? A **road map** could tell you. Road maps show the roads you can use to get from one place to another.

You can find road maps in a highway atlas. You can also buy a road map that shows just one state.

Learn It

Look at the map on page 213. Read the steps for using a road map.

- Read the map title. This map shows some roads in Indiana.

- Look at the map key to understand the symbols. An **interstate highway** connects two or more states. U.S. highways are older roads that pass through towns. A **state highway** begins and ends within a state.

- Identify directions. Roads that run east and west usually have an even number, such as 50 or 70. Roads that run north and south usually have an odd number, such as 69 or 65. This helps drivers figure out in which direction they are driving.

Try It

Use the map on page 213 to answer the questions.

- Which highway could you drive from Gary to Indianapolis?

- Which highway would you take from Indianapolis to visit Hoosier National Forest?

- Which U.S. highway connects South Bend and Indianapolis?

- In which direction does State Highway 50 run?

- Which interstates run east and west, and pass through Indianapolis?

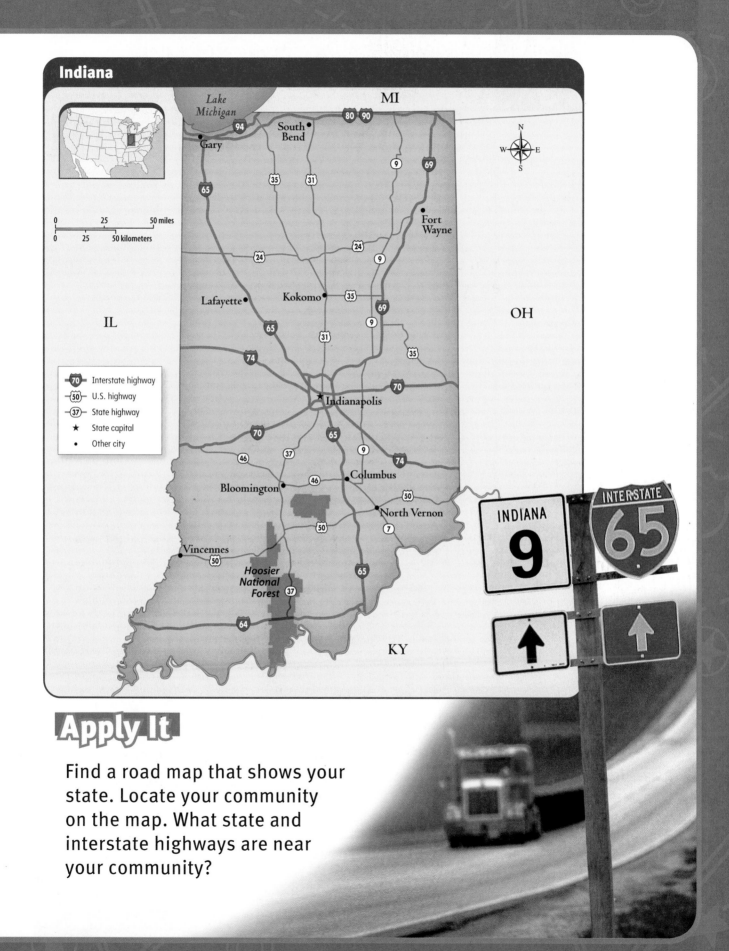

Indiana

Lake Michigan

MI

South Bend

Gary

80 90

9 69

94

35 31

Fort Wayne

65

0 25 50 miles
0 25 50 kilometers

24

IL

Lafayette

Kokomo

35

65

31

74

9

69

9

OH

35

70

70

Indianapolis

★

Interstate highway
U.S. highway
State highway
★ State capital
• Other city

70

65

9

46

37

9

74

Bloomington

46

Columbus

50

North Vernon

Vincennes

50

Hoosier National Forest

37

7

65

50

64

KY

INDIANA
9

INTERSTATE
65

Apply It

Find a road map that shows your state. Locate your community on the map. What state and interstate highways are near your community?

Local Government

VOCABULARY

local government p. 215

mayor p. 215

council p. 216

sovereign p. 219

READING SKILL

Compare and Contrast Copy the diagram below. As you read, use it to show how the jobs of the mayor and city council are alike and different

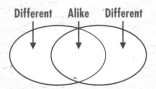

Different   Alike   Different

STANDARDS FOCUS

SOCIAL STUDIES   Individuals, Groups, and Institutions

GEOGRAPHY   Human Systems

Local fire departments help keep communities safe.

Visual Preview

How does local government help the community?

A A mayor and city workers are all part of local government.

B Town and city governments provide many different local services.

C Native American communities have their own local governments.

A CITIES AND TOWNS

Your class is visiting the local firehouse. A loud bell sounds—the firefighters fly into action. With sirens blaring, they climb onto the fire truck and race to the rescue!

Who hires the firefighters and the police? Who makes sure the trash is picked up, and checks that traffic lights work properly? **Local government** does! Local government is the people who run a town or a city. Local government is the level of government that most closely touches our everyday lives.

Let's look at Sylvania, Ohio, to see how its local government works. Craig Stough became **mayor** of Sylvania in 1996. Many towns and cities have a mayor as the head of local government. Each week Mayor Stough goes to meetings, tries to solve city problems, and makes sure city laws are followed. What branch of government does this sound like? If you said the executive branch, you're right!

QUICK CHECK

Compare and Contrast How is a mayor's job different from a governor's job?

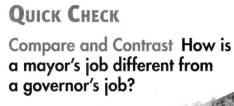

City workers repair streets and roadways. ▶

215

Mayor Stough works with the city **council** to plan for the future of Sylvania. A council is a group of people who make the laws for a community. The council is elected by the citizens of the community. It is the legislative branch of local government. Local governments have a judicial branch, too. The local courts rule on offenses such as traffic tickets.

Community Services Meet Needs

Citizens and businesses pay taxes to local governments. Local governments then use tax money to provide services. They hire people to fix road signs, collect trash and recyclables, and run the library. They pay government employees such as police officers and firefighters. The pictures on the right show some services that most local governments provide.

Towns in other countries have governments, too. You will read about the government of Adelaide, Australia, on page 218.

QUICK CHECK

Compare and Contrast How is a city council different from a state's legislative branch?

The town library provides books, newspapers, and computers.

Police officers keep the community of Sylvania safe.

Firefighters protect Sylvania from fires.

Local government takes care of parks.

The highway department helps keep the roads of Sylvania safe.

Mayor Stough and the Sylvania city council

People visit Sylvania Historical Village to learn about the history of their community.

Global Connections

Local Government of Adelaide, Australia

Back in 1840 the city of Adelaide, Australia, was very small. That was the year the city elected its first mayor. Today Adelaide is one of Australia's largest cities.

Every three years the people of Adelaide elect a mayor and a city council. These government leaders work to keep the city beautiful. The city's many employees take care of Adelaide's libraries, roads, parks, and beaches.

Adelaide is known as "Festival City." Every two years the local government holds the Adelaide Festival of Arts. People from all over the world go to Adelaide for this celebration. Another important Adelaide event is a bicycle race called the Tour Down Under.

Adelaide

▲ Adelaide City Hall

◄ Adelaide's city council sponsors many local events, including a bicycle race.

Write About It Write a paragraph describing how Adelaide's local government is similar to Sylvania's.

Ⓒ NATIVE AMERICAN GOVERNMENT

Native Americans are citizens of two **sovereign** governments—the United States, and their own tribal group, or nation. Sovereign means independent, or self-governing. Native Americans vote in local, state, and national elections. In addition, they may also vote in tribal elections. Each tribal group can make its own laws and choose its own leaders.

There are more than 500 Native American governments in the United States. These governments all share the same goal—they work for their people. For example, the Navajo Nation makes laws that protect Navajo people and Navajo culture.

Tribal governments work with the national, state, and local governments. They also work with other tribal governments and cooperate on many issues that are important to their tribes.

▲ Ben Nighthorse Campbell was a United States senator. Now he serves in the government of the Northern Cheyenne Nation.

QUICK CHECK

Summarize Native Americans are citizens of what governments?

Check Understanding

1. **VOCABULARY** Write one sentence for each of these vocabulary words.
   mayor   council   sovereign

2. **READING SKILL**
   Compare and Contrast
   Use your diagram from page 214 to write a paragraph comparing a mayor and a city council.

   Different   Alike   Different

3. **Write About It** Make a list of some ways people can take part in local government.

Rules and Laws

VOCABULARY

common good p. 222

jury p. 222

Bill of Rights p. 223

READING SKILL

Compare and Contrast
Copy the diagram below. As you read, use it to show how rules are different from laws.

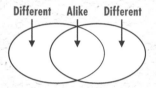

Different   Alike   Different

STANDARDS FOCUS

| SOCIAL STUDIES | Civic Ideals and Practices |

| GEOGRAPHY | Environment and Society |

Rules help keep us safe.

Visual Preview

How does having rules and laws help communities?

A Rules and laws protect us and help us get along.

B Laws are made to protect our rights, and for the good of all.

C Government lawmakers must follow the laws, too.

D Native Americans make laws for their own communities.

RULES AND LAWS HELP PEOPLE

You are at the swimming pool. Your friend wants you to dive in, but just then you see a sign that says "No diving." You know the rule is meant to keep people safe.

Rules not only help keep people safe, rules also help people in a community get along. Have you ever been in a room where everyone was talking at once? It is a lot easier to discuss things when people take turns. Taking turns is a rule that helps people work together.

Laws Are Rules

You know cars must stop at a red light. That's the law. A law is a rule the government makes for all people in a town, state, or country. What would happen if drivers didn't obey this important traffic law? Someone could have an accident, and people might get hurt. If a driver doesn't stop at a red light, a police officer may give the driver a ticket. Then the driver will have to go to court and pay a fine.

Other laws protect our property. For example, it is against the law for someone to take something of yours without permission. People who break laws are punished. They may have to pay a fine or even go to jail.

Rules help us be fair. ▼

QUICK CHECK

Compare and Contrast What would it be like if there were no traffic laws?

B GOOD FOR ALL

Many communities have a law against littering. You might think, "One little wrapper won't matter—I'll just drop it." But what if everyone did that? The streets would be a mess! Putting trash where it belongs is an example of working for the **common good**, or doing whatever helps the most people in the community. Good citizens do things for the common good.

Good Citizens

Governments make laws for the common good. One law says not to chain a bicycle to a fire hydrant. This is for everyone's good, because firefighters need to get to fire hydrants easily. Obeying laws is one way of being a good citizen.

Another way of being a good citizen is to serve on a **jury**. A jury is a group of citizens who listen to the facts in a court trial and make a decision based on the law.

Have you ever voted in a classroom or school election? Good citizens vote for leaders at every level of government—national, state, and local. Voters choose leaders that they believe will work for the common good.

▲ Picking up litter helps everyone.

Voting is one way to be a good citizen. ▼

Register Here

VOTE

Ballots   Ballots

The Bill of Rights protects freedom of speech.

Protecting Rights

The **Bill of Rights** is part of the United States Constitution. It protects our most important rights. In some countries, people can be put in jail just for saying they disagree with the government. In the United States you cannot be arrested for disagreeing. The Bill of Rights makes sure we have the freedom to say and write what we want. It protects other rights, too.

QUICK CHECK

Summarize What are some ways to be a good citizen?

PEOPLE

In the past, African Americans were often treated unfairly. During the 1960s, **Dr. Martin Luther King, Jr.**, led the fight for equal rights for all Americans. Dr. King made speeches and led peaceful marches to help change unfair laws.

Dr. Martin Luther King, Jr.

223

GOVERNMENTS FOLLOW RULES

Good citizens aren't the only ones who follow rules and laws. Governments and government leaders must follow the law, too. The highest, or most important, law in our country is the United States Constitution.

We elect the leaders who will speak and act for us in government. The people who we elect promise to obey the Constitution. This means they cannot pass a law that goes against any laws already in the Constitution.

▼ These lawmakers were elected by members of their communities.

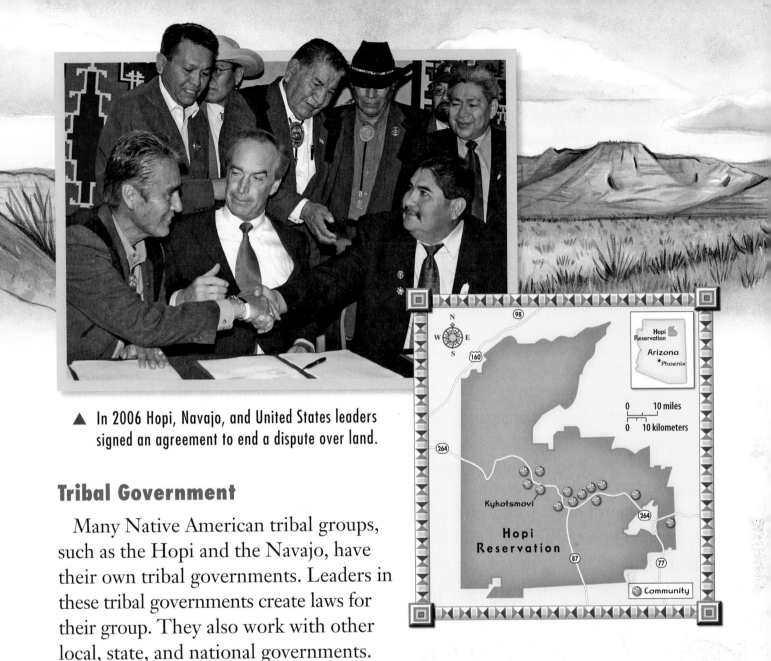

▲ In 2006 Hopi, Navajo, and United States leaders signed an agreement to end a dispute over land.

Tribal Government

Many Native American tribal groups, such as the Hopi and the Navajo, have their own tribal governments. Leaders in these tribal governments create laws for their group. They also work with other local, state, and national governments.

Many Hopi live on the Hopi Reservation in Arizona. A reservation is land set aside for use by Native Americans. The Hopi Tribal Council meets in Kykotsmovi Village, but each of the villages on the reservation also has its own traditional Hopi government. In traditional Hopi government, decisions are not made by voting. Instead problems are discussed until everyone in the community agrees on each decision.

QUICK CHECK

Summarize **Why must governments follow the law?**

Ⓓ HOPI GOVERNMENT

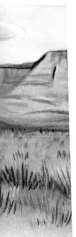

▲ A Hopi police officer on patrol

Each Hopi village sends members to the Hopi Tribal Council. The Council members work for the common good of the Hopi and to help each other in times of need.

A few years ago, the Council formed a water team. The team works with state and national leaders to protect Hopi water rights. Hopi Tribal Chairman Wayne Taylor, Jr., said,

❝Of all the [things] necessary for economic development, none is more important than water. . . .❞

QUICK CHECK

Summarize **What does the Hopi Tribal Council do?**

Check Understanding

1. **VOCABULARY** Write a sentence to explain each vocabulary term.
   common good   **Bill of Rights**

2. **READING SKILL**
   Compare and Contrast
   Use your diagram from page 220 to write a paragraph describing how rules are different from laws.

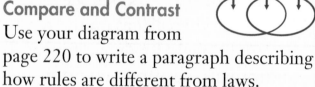
Different Alike Different

3. **Write About It** Write a paragraph about some of the things people in your community do that are for the common good.

EXPLORE The Big Idea

Citizenship

Democracy in Action

Being Informed

Students in Claysville, Pennsylvania, noticed a lot of trash outside their school. No wonder! There were no trash cans! The class decided to do something. They found out who to ask for help and how to get what they wanted. Now the playground is cleaner. Read the steps below to learn how to become informed.

Being Informed

1. **Identify the problem.** Make a list of what you already know, and what you need to find out.

2. **Get information.** Read local newspapers, search the Internet, watch television, or talk to people who know about the problem.

3. **Examine the information.** Try to decide which information is fact and which is opinion.

4. **Find out who is in charge.** Some problems are the responsibility of government leaders. Find out which leader is in charge of the problem you're interested in.

Write About It Gather information about a problem in your school or community. Write a paragraph telling what you think should be done.

Taking Action

Lesson 5

VOCABULARY

volunteer p. 229

nonprofit p. 230

bill p. 231

READING SKILL

Compare and Contrast
Copy the diagram below. As you read, list how lawmakers and volunteers are alike and different.

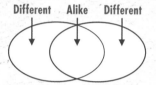

STANDARDS FOCUS

SOCIAL STUDIES Individual Development and Identity

GEOGRAPHY Environment and Society

A beautiful community makes everyone happy.

Visual Preview

What are some ways people get involved in their community?

A People can do many things to help their community.

B Some people work with others to help people in their community.

C People vote for lawmakers who will best help their community.

D Voting is the right of every United States citizen.

GETTING INVOLVED

People in your neighborhood have permission to turn an empty lot into a little park. Everyone works on the clean-up. You offer to help paint a mural for the new park.

If you **volunteer** to help, you are being a good citizen. A volunteer is a person who chooses to do a job without getting paid. Volunteers do many things. They might clean a park or collect clothing for the homeless. They work for the common good of their community.

What Can People Do to Help?

People can volunteer to do many different things. Volunteers who clean up public parks make them better for everyone. Some people collect canned food to help people who do not have enough to eat. Planting flowers can make a community more beautiful. In some schools, volunteers help other students with their schoolwork.

EVENT

National & Global Youth Service Day teaches children the importance of volunteering. Young people can volunteer to pick up trash, clean schools, or teach others about the environment.

National & Global Youth Service Day

QUICK CHECK

Compare and Contrast **How is a volunteer different from an employee?**

People often volunteer by joining **nonprofit** groups. A nonprofit group does not make money from the work it does. The Red Cross is a nonprofit group that helps communities during disasters, such as hurricanes or tornadoes.

In 2005 Jackie, Melissa, and Jenna Kantor were just 14, 11, and 8 years old. They decided to help families affected by Hurricane Katrina. They started Project Backpack. They collected school supplies, toys, and books and sent them in backpacks to kids who needed help.

Building Homes

Habitat for Humanity is a nonprofit group that helps people build homes for themselves. Families who need houses work with Habitat volunteers to build their own homes. This nonprofit group allows people in a community to help their neighbors.

▲ Kids started a nonprofit group called Project Backpack.

▼ Habitat for Humanity volunteers help build houses.

Make a Difference

Have you ever wondered if you can really make a difference? You can—no matter how old you are. In New Hampshire, a group of third and fourth graders wrote a **bill** saying that the pumpkin should be the state fruit. A bill is a written idea for a law. Why did they choose the pumpkin? Student Reanna Parker said, "It's strong and sturdy like the people of New Hampshire."

The students got their representative in the state government to present the bill to other lawmakers. In April 2006, the New Hampshire House of Representatives and Senate made the bill a law.

▲ Third and fourth graders took their idea to state lawmakers.

Children in Illinois wanted to make a difference in another way. They held car washes and ran bake sales to raise money for hurricane victims. One school raised over $5,000 by selling lemonade! The kids who worked on these projects felt great knowing that their actions made a difference to people who needed help.

QUICK CHECK

Summarize **How do people make a difference in their communities?**

231

GOVERNMENT LEADERS HELP

Have you ever dreamed of running for government office? You can start by getting involved in your school government. As you grow up, you can stay involved in government. Being a government leader is one way people help their community.

United States Senator Blanche Lincoln is from Arkansas. She works to make laws that will aid people in her state. Senator Lincoln is interested in helping farmers and other people who live in rural areas of Arkansas. The senator also works hard for children in her state. She has helped pass laws to be sure all children have good health care and enough to eat.

▲ Arkansas Senator Blanche Lincoln

▼ Lawmakers make sure students can eat a healthy lunch.

Get Out and Vote

As you have learned, government leaders such as Senator Lincoln are elected by the people. If people think Senator Lincoln does a good job, they let her know by voting for her again. If you are a citizen, one day you will be able to vote. The people you vote for will make the laws that affect you.

In the past, not everyone could vote. When the Constitution was first written in 1789, only white men were allowed to vote. Read on to find out how voting rights have changed since then.

▲ Some government leaders help support after-school sports programs.

PEOPLE

Government leaders volunteer, too. **Jimmy Carter** was our President from 1977 to 1981. Now he works with Habitat for Humanity. He also works for better health care around the world.

President Jimmy Carter

QUICK CHECK

Main Idea and Details **How do government leaders help communities?**

1848 Elizabeth Cady Stanton and Lucretia Mott leads a meeting in New York, called the Seneca Falls Convention, to discuss women's rights.

1870 The Fifteenth Amendment gives African American men the right to vote.

Ⓓ HISTORY OF VOTING RIGHTS

In the late 1700s, when the United States government was just beginning, only white men could vote. African American men and all women were not allowed to vote. They did not have a say in how the government was run. People worked hard to change this, and over the years, more and more people won the right to vote.

Fighting for Change

In 1866 Elizabeth Cady Stanton and Susan B. Anthony formed the American Equal Rights Association. This group worked to win the right to vote for all men and women. Soon other groups formed. They tried to convince the government to change the laws. People made signs and organized meetings and parades. Some even went to jail for their actions.

1920 The Nineteenth Amendment gives women the right to vote.

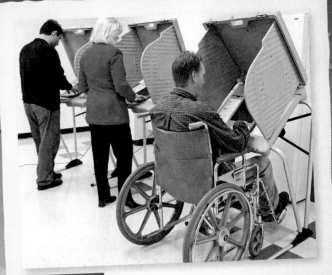

Today Today every United States citizen who is eighteen or older has the right to vote.

Voting Today

It took many years, but the law was finally changed. The United States Constitution was amended, or changed, to include more people who could vote. Today it is against the law to prevent any citizen from voting.

QUICK CHECK

Compare and Contrast **How is voting today different than voting before 1870?**

Check Understanding

1. **VOCABULARY** Write three or four sentences explaining ways to be a good citizen. Use these vocabulary words.
   volunteer   **nonprofit**

2. **READING SKILL**
   Compare and Contrast
   Use your diagram from page 228 to write a paragraph on how volunteers and lawmakers are alike and different.

   Different Alike Different

3. **Write About It** Write a letter to your local government about a change you would like to see in your community.

Local Connections

Symbols and Landmarks in Your Community

Nadia lives in St. Louis, Missouri. She learned about her community's symbols, landmarks, and city seal. Then she decided to make her own city seal. You can make a city seal for your community, too. Here is what to do:

- Go to your city hall, your local library, or look on the Internet to find out about your city or town's seal and local landmarks.

- Think about other people, places, or things that are symbols of your community. Which of these could you put on a seal? What is your city known for? What animals live nearby? Were any famous people born in your community? What is produced in your area?

- Find photographs of your community's symbols and landmarks that will help you make your own city seal.

For more help with your project visit
www.macmillanmh.com

Government Activity

Make a City Seal

1 Look at your notes and pictures. Choose one or more things you would like to put on your city seal.

2 Try out many ideas on notebook paper until you make a design you really like. Some city seals show just one place or thing. Others include three or four symbols.

3 Draw your best design on poster board.

4 Include your city's name on your seal. You may also want to include the year it was founded, or a nickname for the city.

5 Share your city seal with your classmates.

Materials
- photographs
- notebook
- markers, colored pencils, or crayons
- poster board

Unit 5   Review and Assess

Vocabulary

Write the sentences. Choose the correct term to fill in the blank.

governor   **Bill of Rights**

council   **nonprofit**

1. The town _____ makes laws in local government.
2. The ___ is part of the Constitution.
3. The head of a state's executive branch is the _____.
4. Many people volunteer to work for a _____ group such as the Red Cross.

Comprehension and Critical Thinking

5. What are the five basic rights protected by the Constitution?
6. What is an example of something that is done for the common good?
7. **Reading Skill** Why might local government affect citizens more than state or national governments do?
8. **Critical Thinking** Why is it important to vote?

Skill

Use Road Maps

Write a complete sentence to answer each question.

9. What kind of road is Highway 84?
10. Which roads would you drive on if you traveled from Enfield to New Haven to Norwalk?

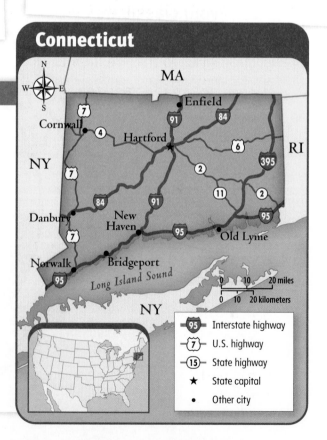

Connecticut

 # Test Preparation

Study the flow chart. Then answer the questions.

An Idea Becomes a United States Law

People get an idea for a new law. They get their representative to support the idea.

A representative presents the idea to Congress as a bill.

Members of Congress vote on the bill. If enough vote yes, the bill passes.

If the bill passes, the President may sign the bill into law.

1. What is the first step for citizens to get a new law passed?

   A. They write to the President.

   B. They get an idea and tell their representative.

   C. They talk about their idea on television.

   D. They send their idea to the local newspaper.

2. To whom does the representative present the bill?

   A. the newspaper

   B. the President

   C. the mayor

   D. Congress

3. A bill becomes United States law when it is signed by

   A. the President.

   B. the governor.

   C. the city council.

   D. citizens.

4. What could citizens do if Congress does not vote yes to pass the bill?

5. What things might a member of Congress think about before he or she voted yes to a bill?

239

Why do communities need governments?

Write About the Big Idea

Write an Essay

Think about what you have learned in Unit 5. Use your foldable to help you write an essay that answers the Big Idea question. First write an introduction. Then write one paragraph about each level of government. Tell what the government does at each level, and explain why communities need government. For local government, include examples from your own local government. Then write a conclusion to your essay.

FOLDABLES™
Study Organizer

Levels of Government
National

State

Local

Projects About the Big Idea

Plan a School Project Think about your school community. Is everything just the way you want it, or is there something you would like to change? Work with other students to plan a project that will bring about a change for the common good.

Make a Poster Make a poster that shows the elected members of your local government. Include the services your local government provides to your community.

Reference Section

Main Idea and Details

The **main idea** is what the paragraph is about. It is what the author wants you to understand about the subject. Often the main idea is in the first sentence of a paragraph. The other sentences have **details** that tell more about the main idea. Finding the main idea and details will help you understand what you read.

Learn It

- **Read the paragraph.** Think about what the paragraph is about. See if there is a sentence which states the main idea.

- **Now look for details.** Sentences with details give more information about the main idea.

Main Idea The first sentence states the main idea.	There are many interesting things to do in Pittsburgh. If you are interested in science, you can go to the Carnegie Science center. There you can board a real submarine. If you like animals you can visit the zoo. You can visit the Children's Museum where you can work with paint and clay.
Details These details tell some of the fun things to do in Pittsburgh.	

Try It

Copy and complete the chart. Write the main idea and the details of the paragraph on page 1 in the boxes.

Main Idea	Details

Apply It

- Review the steps in Learn It.

- Read the paragraph below. Then make a main idea and details chart for the paragraph.

It takes many people to build a new building. An architect makes a plan that tells how the building will be made. Steelworkers put up the framework. Other workers pour concrete. Others may lay bricks to make the walls. Electricians put in wires and lighting.

Unit 2 • Reading Skills

Sequence

The paragraph below tells some events during Christopher Columbus's first journey to the Americas. When you read, think about the **sequence**, or order, of events. Thinking about the order of events will help you understand and remember what you read.

Learn It

- Look for clue words such as first, next, later, and last. These words can help show the order of events.

- Look for dates that tell exactly when things happened.

First Event
Columbus left Spain.

Clue words
These words help you recognize other events. sequence.

Dates
Dates help you keep events in order.

Christopher Columbus and his crew left Spain on August 3, 1492. The first stop was the Canary Islands. There they got fresh supplies. Five weeks later, Columbus and his crew landed on an island in what is now the Bahamas. Both Columbus and his crew were glad to be on land! Next, Columbus explored the coast of Cuba and the coast of Hispaniola. By January 1493, Columbus began sailing back to Spain.

Try It

Copy and complete the chart below. Write the events from the paragraph on page 1 in the correct sequence. You may need to add boxes to the chart to show more events.

First
↓
Next
↓
Last

How did you figure out the sequence of events?

Apply It

- Review the sequencing steps in Learn It.

- Read the paragraph below. Then create a sequence of events chart to show the order of events.

In August 1620 the Pilgrims left England to go to America. They started out on two ships, the Speedwell and the Mayflower. The Speedwell began leaking, so both ships returned to land. All the Pilgrims crowded onto the Mayflower. The Pilgrims began their journey once again. They sailed for many weeks. On November 11th, the Mayflower reached America.

Summarize

How do you tell a friend about a book or movie? You might retell the story in your own words. Of course, you don't tell every single thing that happened. You tell the important parts. To retell a story this way is to summarize. **Summarizing** what you have read can help you remember information in social studies.

Learn It

- Read the whole selection. Try to state what the selection is about in your own words.

- Find important supporting details and combine them.

- Write one or two sentences to summarize what the whole selection is telling you.

Details
These details support the main idea. They can be combined.

Main Idea
This is a main idea. Use it to begin your summary.

Some holidays honor heroes, such as Martin Luther King, Jr. Others are special to the different ethnic groups in our country. For example, Irish Americans wear green to honor St. Patrick on St. Patrick's Day. Mexican Americans celebrate Cinco de Mayo. Some holidays honor Americans who fought in wars to defend our country. Veteran's Day, November 11, honors people who served in our armed forces. On Memorial Day, we remember men and women who died in wars. There are many reasons Americans celebrate holidays.

Try It

Now copy the chart. Fill in the boxes to summarize the paragraphs on page R6.

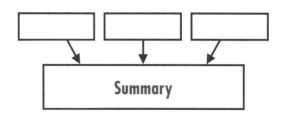

Write a summary of the selection on page R6.

Apply It

- Review the summarizing steps in Learn It.

- Make a chart like the one above. Use it to summarize the paragraphs below.

People in Barbourville, Kentucky, hold a Daniel Boone Festival to honor the explorer Daniel Boone. The festival has a parade, a fishing competition, and a quilt show. The town of Akeley, Minnesota, has a celebration called Paul Bunyan Days to honor the legend of Paul Bunyan.

Mark Twain was an American writer. People in Hannibal, Missouri, hold a festival to celebrate his stories, called National Tom Sawyer Days. It is named for character in one of Twain's books. During the festival there is a fence-painting contest and a frog-jumping contest.

Cause and Effect

Think about the last time you spent money. You had a reason. A **cause**, or reason, is why something happens. An **effect** is what happens. Thinking about causes and effects will help you understand events you read about.

Learn It

- To find a cause, ask, "Why did it happen?"

- To find an effect, ask, "What happened?"

- Look for words such as because, as a result, and so. These words often link causes and effects.

- Now look for causes and effects in the paragraph.

Cause
This sentence tells why Ana had money.

Effect
This is an effect.

Clue words
The words "as a result" and "so" are clue words. These words often link causes and effects.

Ana's grandparents and aunts gave her money for her birthday this year. As a result, Ana has $70. She decided to save $50 of the money, so she opened a savings account. So now she has $20 left to spend on things she wants.

Try It

Copy the cause and effect chart below. Then complete the chart with causes and effects from the paragraph on page R8.

Cause	→	Effect
	→	
	→	
	→	

Apply It

• Review the steps for understanding cause and effect in Learn It.

• Read the paragraph below. Then make a chart to show the two causes and two effects.

Because he wanted to buy something special, Danny saved all the money he made delivering newspapers. He wants to get a new computer game. He'd like a new baseball glove, too. Danny only has enough money for one or the other. So he needs to make a decision.

Unit 5 • Reading Skills
Compare and Contrast

Compare means to see how things are alike.
Contrast means to see how things are different.
Comparing and contrasting will help you understand
what you read in social studies.

Learn It

- To compare two things, look for how they are alike.

- To contrast two things, look for ways they are
  different.

  Now read the passage below. Think about how the
  Washington Monument and the Lincoln Memorial
  are alike and different.

Alike
Both honor Presidents.
Both are on the Mall.

The Washington Monument and the Lincoln
Memorial honor two of our country's greatest
Presidents. Both structures are located on the
Mall in Washington, D.C. and both are famous
buildings. The Lincoln Memorial is a low,
wide building. It has a large statue of
Abraham Lincoln inside. The Washington
Monument looks like a tall needle. There is
no statue of Washington in the building. The
building does have an elevator that carries
visitors 500 feet to the top so they can look
out over the city.

Different
The Lincoln Memorial is a wide, low building. It has a statue of Lincoln.
The Washington Monument is tall. It does not have a statue.

Try It

Copy the Venn Diagram. Then fill in the left-hand side with details about the Washington Monument. Fill in the right side with details about the Lincoln Memorial. Fill in the center with ways the two buildings are alike.

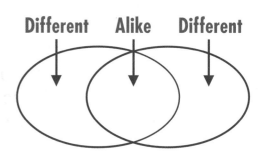

What did you look for to find how they were alike and different?

Apply It

- Review the steps for comparing and contrasting in Learn It.

- Read the paragraph below. Then make a Venn Diagram to compare and contrast the two eagles.

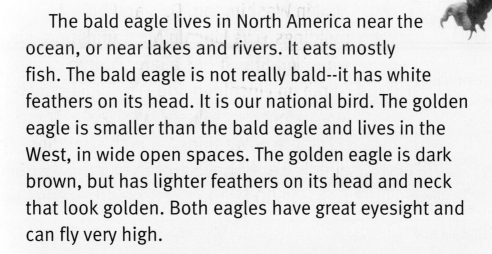

The bald eagle lives in North America near the ocean, or near lakes and rivers. It eats mostly fish. The bald eagle is not really bald--it has white feathers on its head. It is our national bird. The golden eagle is smaller than the bald eagle and lives in the West, in wide open spaces. The golden eagle is dark brown, but has lighter feathers on its head and neck that look golden. Both eagles have great eyesight and can fly very high.

Geography Handbook

Geography and You

Geography is the study of Earth and the people, plants, and animals that live on it. Most people think of geography as learning about cities, states, and countries, but geography is far more. Geography includes learning about land—mountains, and plains—and bodies of water—oceans, lakes, and rivers.

Geography includes the study of how people adapt to living in a new place. Geography is about how people move around, how they move goods, and how ideas travel from place to place.

Geography includes so many things that geographers have divided this information into six elements, or ideas, so you can better understand them.

Six Essential Elements

The World in Spatial Terms: Where is a place located and what land or water features does this place have?

Places and Regions: What is special about a place and what makes it different from another place?

Physical Systems: What has shaped the land and climate of a place, and how does this affect the plants, animals, and people there?

Human Systems: How do people, ideas, and goods move from place to place?

Environment and Society: How have people changed the land and water of a place, and how have the land and water affected the people of a place?

Uses of Geography: How does geography influence events of the past, present, and future?

Five Themes of Geography

You have just read about six essential elements. The five themes of geography are another way to divide the ideas of geography. These themes are location, place, region, movement, and human interaction. They help us think about the world around us. Look for these themes as you read the Map Skill questions throughout the book.

1. Location

The White House

In geography, location means an exact spot on the planet. A location often means a street name and number, such as 1600 Pennsylvania Avenue, the address of the White House. You write a location when you address a letter.

2. Place

Chicago, Illinois

What makes one place different from another? Every place has physical and human features such as mountains or lakes, that describe it. Place also includes human features such as where people live, how they work, and what languages they speak.

3. Region

The Arizona desert

A region is a larger area than a place or location. A region is an area with common features that set it apart from other areas. One region may have many mountains or be mostly desert. People in a region may share customs and language.

4. Movement

Throughout history people have moved things and themselves from one place to another. Geographers study why these movements happen. They also look at how people's movement changes an area.

5. Human Interaction

The Hoover Dam

Geographers study how people adapt to their environment. They also study how people change their environment. They build bridges to make travel easier, or build dams to store water and make electricity.

Dictionary of Geographic Terms

1. **BAY** Body of water partly surrounded by land
2. **BEACH** Land covered with sand or pebbles next to an ocean or lake
3. **CANAL** Waterway dug across the land to connect two bodies of water
4. **CANYON** Deep river valley with steep sides
5. **CLIFF** High steep face of rock
6. **COAST** Land next to an ocean

7. **DESERT** A dry environment with few plants and animals
8. **GULF** Body of water partly surrounded by land; larger than a bay
9. **HARBOR** Protected place by an ocean or river where ships can safely stay
10. **HILL** Rounded, raised landform; not as high as a mountain

ISLAND Land that is surrounded on all sides by water

12 **LAKE** Body of water completely surrounded by land	**17** **PLAIN** Large area of flat land
13 **MESA** Landform that looks like a high, flat table	**18** **PLATEAU** High flat area that rises steeply above the surrounding land
14 **MOUNTAIN** High landform with steep sides; higher than a hill	**19** **PORT** Place where ships load and unload goods
15 **OCEAN** Large body of salt water	**20** **RIVER** Long stream of water that empties into another body of water
16 **PENINSULA** Land that has water on all sides but one	**21** **VALLEY** Area of low land between hills or mountains

Looking at Earth
Earth and the Globe

From outer space, Earth looks like a big blue ball with green and brown areas of land and white clouds. A globe is a model of Earth. It shows what the land and water look like on Earth.

You can see a line around the widest part of the globe. This is the equator. The equator is an imaginary line that separates the north from the south.

The farthest point north on the globe is called the North Pole. The farthest point south on the globe is called the South Pole.

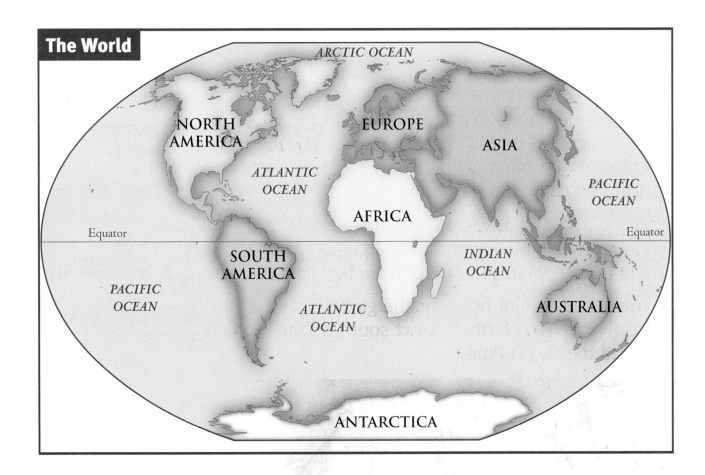

The World

ARCTIC OCEAN

NORTH AMERICA

EUROPE

ASIA

ATLANTIC OCEAN

PACIFIC OCEAN

AFRICA

Equator

Equator

SOUTH AMERICA

INDIAN OCEAN

PACIFIC OCEAN

ATLANTIC OCEAN

AUSTRALIA

ANTARCTICA

A Map of the World

A world map is a flat drawing of Earth. This map shows the continents and the oceans. Unlike a globe, a flat map can be used in a book.

The big areas of land on the Earth are called continents. The big bodies of water are called oceans.

There are seven continents on Earth. There are four major oceans. The equator divides the Earth into the northern half and the southern half.

What are the seven continents of the world?

What are the four oceans?

Reading a Map

A map is a drawing of a place. Some maps show only part of the world. This map shows the United States. Most maps have features that help us read and use maps. Some map features are called out here.

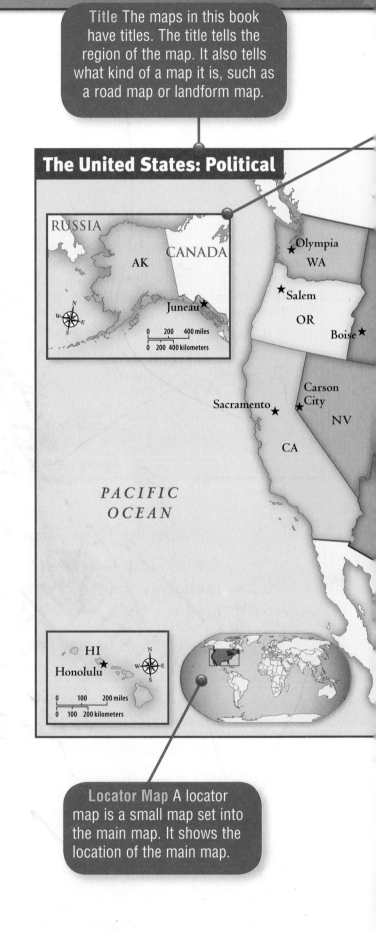

Title The maps in this book have titles. The title tells the region of the map. It also tells what kind of a map it is, such as a road map or landform map.

The United States: Political

RUSSIA

CANADA

AK

Juneau★

0 200 400 miles
0 200 400 kilometers

★Olympia
WA

★Salem

OR

Boise ★

Carson
★City

Sacramento ★

NV

CA

PACIFIC
OCEAN

HI
Honolulu ★

0 100 200 miles
0 100 200 kilometers

Locator Map A locator map is a small map set into the main map. It shows the location of the main map.

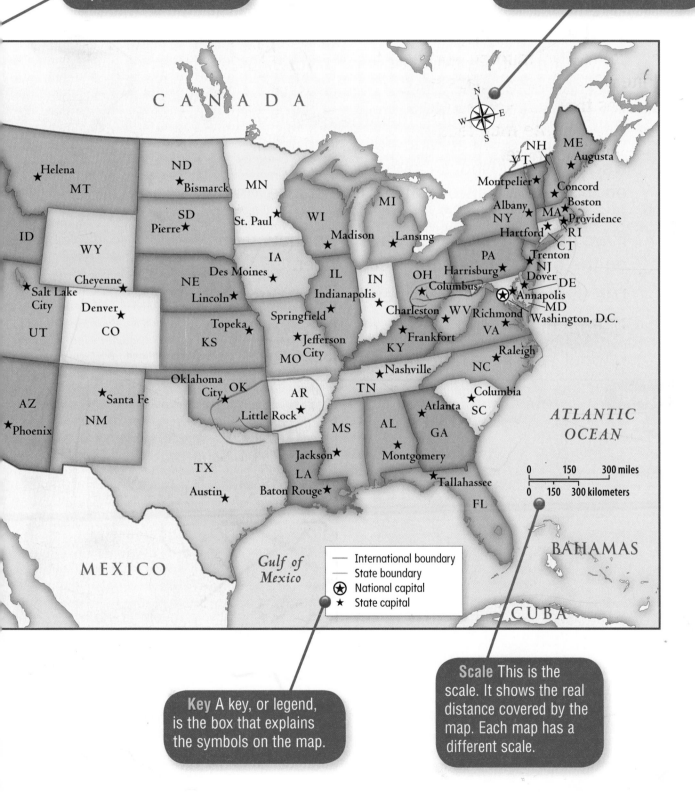

Inset Map An inset map is a small map. It shows an area that is too large, too small, or too far away to include on the main map.

Compass Rose A compass rose shows where north, south, east, and west are on the map.

Key A key, or legend, is the box that explains the symbols on the map.

Scale This is the scale. It shows the real distance covered by the map. Each map has a different scale.

CANADA

Helena
MT
ND
Bismarck
MN
MI
NH ME
Augusta
VT
Montpelier
Concord
Boston
SD
Pierre
St. Paul
WI
Madison
Lansing
Albany
NY MA
Providence
Hartford
RI
CT
ID
WY
Cheyenne
IA
Des Moines
NE
Lincoln
IL
Springfield
IN
Indianapolis
OH
Columbus
PA
Harrisburg
Trenton
NJ
Dover
DE
Salt Lake City
Denver
CO
Topeka
KS
Jefferson City
MO
Charleston
WV
Richmond
Annapolis
MD
Washington, D.C.
VA
UT
Santa Fe
Oklahoma City
OK
AR
Little Rock
KY
Frankfort
Nashville
TN
Raleigh
NC
Columbia
SC
AZ
NM
Phoenix
MS
Jackson
AL
Montgomery
GA
Atlanta
ATLANTIC OCEAN
TX
Austin
LA
Baton Rouge
Tallahassee
FL

Gulf of Mexico

MEXICO

BAHAMAS

CUBA

	International boundary
	State boundary
⊛	National capital
★	State capital

0   150   300 miles
0   150   300 kilometers

Finding Distance and Direction

To find direction on a map we use a compass rose. It shows the directions north, south, east, and west.

• If you travel from New London to Norwich, in what direction do you go?

A map is always smaller than the real place it represents. To understand how much smaller, we use a scale. A scale shows how much a certain distance on the map equals on Earth. For instance, on this map, one inch represents 20 miles on the real Earth. If we use the scale we can figure out how far places on the map really are from each other.

Use the map scale to answer the questions.

• About how far is it from Danbury to Waterbury?

• About how far is it from New Haven to Norwich?

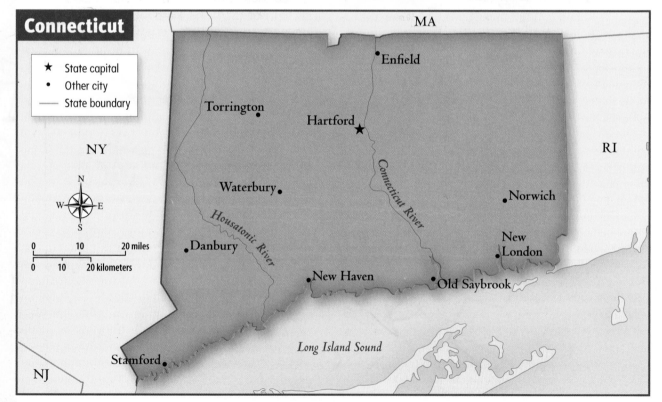

Connecticut

★ State capital
• Other city
— State boundary

MA
Enfield
Torrington
Hartford ★
NY
Waterbury
Connecticut River
Housatonic River
Norwich
RI
Danbury
New London
New Haven
Old Saybrook
Stamford
Long Island Sound
NJ

N
W—E
S

0   10   20 miles
0 10   20 kilometers

Special Maps

Maps can show many different kinds of information. Here are some kinds of special maps.

[B head] Landform Map

Landforms are different types of land on Earth. Mountains, hills, and deserts are all landforms. This map shows the landforms of Pennsylvania. You need to use the map key to understand what the the different colors on the map mean.

• Look at the map key. What does the color red show?

• What color is used for hills?

• On what kind of landform is Philadelphia located?

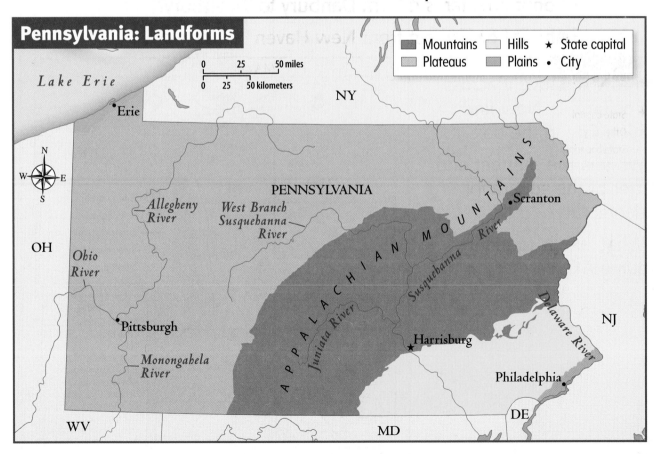

Pennsylvania: Landforms

Mountains Hills ★ State capital
Plateaus Plains • City

Lake Erie

NY

• Erie

PENNSYLVANIA

Allegheny River

West Branch Susquehanna River

A P P A L A C H I A N   M O U N T A I N S

• Scranton

Susquehanna River

OH

Ohio River

Juniata River

• Pittsburgh

★ Harrisburg

Delaware River

NJ

Monongahela River

Philadelphia

DE

WV

MD

Road Map/Grid Map

A road map, sometimes called a route map, shows roads and highways. You would use a road map if you wanted to find know which road to take to go from one city to another, or from one state to another. This map shows the roads in New Jersey.

Grid maps help you locate exact areas. A grid map uses a pattern of lines that form boxes, or a grid. Each box is named using a letter and a number.

The map of New Jersey has a grid on it. Look at the key. The key helps you find things on the map. For instance, the key shows you that Union City is in box A2. To find Union City, put your finger on row A. Move it across to column 2. Now find Union City in the box.

• What is the number and letter of the square for Atlantic City?

• What lake is found in square A1?

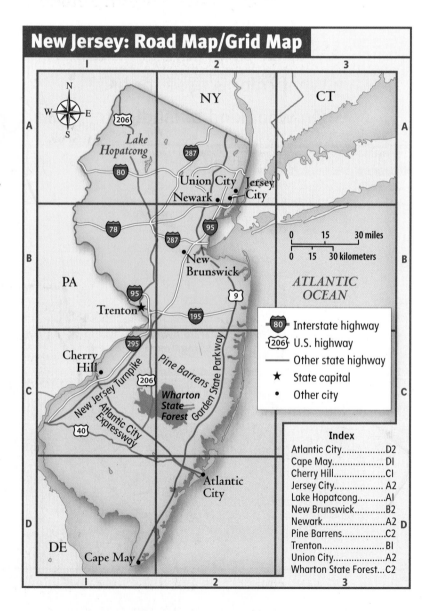

New Jersey: Road Map/Grid Map

NY
CT
PA
ATLANTIC OCEAN
DE

0   15   30 miles
0   15   30 kilometers

80 Interstate highway
206 U.S. highway
— Other state highway
★ State capital
• Other city

Historical Maps

A historical map shows how a place appeared at a certain time in the past. Use the key to understand symbols and colors on the map. The key gives details about the time in history. This map shows how our country looked when people from Europe first moved here. It shows the first thirteen colonies.

• What colonies were called the southern colonies?

• What city was a Pilgrim settlement?

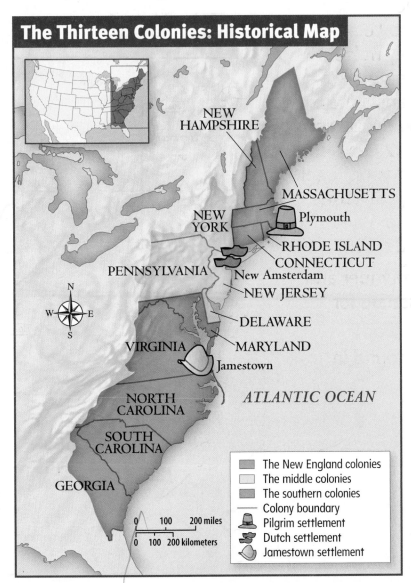

The Thirteen Colonies: Historical Map

NEW HAMPSHIRE

MASSACHUSETTS

Plymouth

NEW YORK

RHODE ISLAND

CONNECTICUT

New Amsterdam

PENNSYLVANIA

NEW JERSEY

DELAWARE

MARYLAND

VIRGINIA

Jamestown

ATLANTIC OCEAN

NORTH CAROLINA

SOUTH CAROLINA

GEORGIA

0   100   200 miles

0   100 200 kilometers

The New England colonies
The middle colonies
The southern colonies
Colony boundary
Pilgrim settlement
Dutch settlement
Jamestown settlement

United States: Political

ARCTIC OCEAN

RUSSIA

CANADA

Nome · *Yukon River* · Fairbanks

ALASKA

Anchorage ·

Juneau ★

| 0 | 200 | 400 miles |
| 0 | 200 | 400 kilometers |

Seattle ·
Olympia ★
Spokane ·
WASHINGTON

Portland ·
Salem ★
Eugene ·
OREGON

Great Falls ·
Missouri River
Helena ★ MONTANA
Billings ·

IDAHO
Boise ★
Pocatello ·

WYOMING
Casper ·
Cheyenne ★

Eureka ·
Redding ·

Great Salt Lake
Ogden ·
Salt Lake City ★ Provo ·

Reno ·
Carson City ★
NEVADA

UTAH

Denver ★
COLORADO
Colorado Springs ·
Pueblo ·

Sacramento ★
San Francisco ·
Oakland ·
San Jose ·
Fresno ·

CALIFORNIA

Las Vegas ·
Colorado River

Bakersfield ·

Santa Fe ★
Albuquerque ·

Los Angeles ·
Long Beach ·

San Diego ·

ARIZONA
Phoenix ★

NEW MEXICO

Tucson ·

El Paso ·
Rio Grande

PACIFIC OCEAN

| 0 | 200 | 400 miles |
| 0 | 200 | 400 kilometers |

Gulf of California

MEXICO

Kauai
Oahu
HAWAII
Niihau
Honolulu ★ Molokai
PACIFIC OCEAN
Lanai
Maui
Kahoolawe
Hilo ·
Hawaii

| 0 | 100 | 200 miles |
| 0 | 100 | 200 kilometers |

⊛	International boundary
	State boundary
⊛	National capital
★	State capital
·	Other city

CANADA

NORTH DAKOTA
Grand Forks
Fargo
Bismarck

SOUTH DAKOTA
Pierre

MINNESOTA
Duluth
St. Paul
Minneapolis

Marquette

Lake Superior

MICHIGAN

Green Bay
WISCONSIN
Milwaukee
Madison
Grand Rapids
Lansing

Lake Huron

Lake Michigan

Lake Ontario
Lake Erie
Detroit
Toledo Cleveland

NEW HAMPSHIRE
VERMONT
Montpelier
MAINE
Augusta
Portland
Concord

Albany
Boston
MASSACHUSETTS

NEW YORK
Buffalo
Hartford
Providence
RHODE ISLAND
CONNECTICUT

Sioux Falls

IOWA
Cedar Rapids

Chicago

Gary

PENNSYLVANIA
Harrisburg
Newark
New York
Trenton
NEW JERSEY

NEBRASKA
Omaha
Lincoln

Missouri River

Des Moines

ILLINOIS
Davenport

OHIO
Columbus

INDIANA

Pittsburgh
Baltimore
Philadelphia
Dover
DELAWARE

Topeka
KANSAS

Kansas City
Kansas City

St. Louis
Jefferson City

Springfield
Indianapolis
Cincinnati

Evansville

Ohio River
Louisville
Frankfort
KENTUCKY

WEST VIRGINIA
Charleston
VIRGINIA

Washington, DC
Annapolis
MARYLAND

Richmond
Norfolk

Wichita

MISSOURI

Tulsa

Oklahoma City
OKLAHOMA

Fort Smith
ARKANSAS
Little Rock

Nashville
TENNESSEE
Tennessee River
Memphis

Knoxville
NORTH CAROLINA
Raleigh
Charlotte

Columbia
SOUTH CAROLINA

Charleston

Brazos River

TEXAS

Dallas
Fort Worth

Austin
San Antonio
Houston

Laredo
Corpus Christi

Mississippi River

Shreveport

LOUISIANA
Baton Rouge
New Orleans

MISSISSIPPI
Jackson

Birmingham
ALABAMA
Montgomery

Mobile
Biloxi

GEORGIA
Columbus

Atlanta

Savannah

Jacksonville
Tallahassee

ATLANTIC OCEAN

Orlando
FLORIDA
Tampa

Miami

Gulf of Mexico

BAHAMAS

N
W   E
S

CUBA

GH15

United States: Physical

ARCTIC OCEAN

RUSSIA

BROOKS RANGE
ALASKA

Arctic Circle

CANADA

Bering Strait

Mt. McKinley
20,320 ft.
(6,194 m)

Yukon River

ALASKA RANGE

Bering
Sea

Gulf of Alaska

N
W E
S

Aleutian Islands

0   200   400 miles
0   200   400 kilometers

PACIFIC OCEAN

International
boundary
▲ Mountain peak
▲ Highest point
▼ Lowest point

HAWAII

Kauai

Niihau

Oahu

N
W E
S

Molokai

PACIFIC
OCEAN

Lanai

Maui

Kahoolawe

Hawaii

Mauna Kea
13,796 ft.
(4,205 m)

0   100   200 miles
0   100   200 kilometers

Puget
Sound

Mt. Rainier
14,410 ft. (4,392 m) ▲

Mt. St. Helens
8,363 ft. (2,549 m)

Columbia R.

Mt. Hood
11,239 ft.
(3,426 m)

ROCKY

Missouri River

Mt. Shasta
14,162 ft.
(4,317 m)

CASCADE RANGE

COLUMBIA PLATEAU

Snake River

Granite Peak
12,799 ft.
(3,901 m)

BLAC
HILL

Cape
Mendocino

SIERRA NEVADA

CENTRAL VALLEY

Sacramento R.

Great Salt
Lake

GREAT
BASIN

WASATCH RANGE

Kings Peak
13,528 ft.
(4,123 m)

M
O
U
N
T
A
I
N
S

Mt. Elbert
14,433 ft.
(4,399 m)

Lake
Tahoe

GREAT
SALT LAKE
DESERT

San Francisco
Bay

San Joaquin R.

COASTRANGES

Mt. Whitney
14,494 ft.
(4,418 m)

COLORADO

PLATEAU

Pikes Peak
14,110 ft.
(4,301 m)

Lake
Mead

Death Valley
-282 ft.
(-86 m)

PACIFIC
OCEAN

Channel
Islands

Salton
Sea

MOJAVE
DESERT

Colorado River

Humphreys Peak
12,633 ft.
(3,851 m)

CONTINENTAL DIVIDE

Wheeler Pe
13,161 ft.
(4,011 m)

Pecos River

Gila River

SONORAN
DESERT

Guadalupe
8,749 ft.
(2,667 m)

Rio Grande

Gulf of California

MEXICO

0   200   400 miles
0   200   400 kilometers

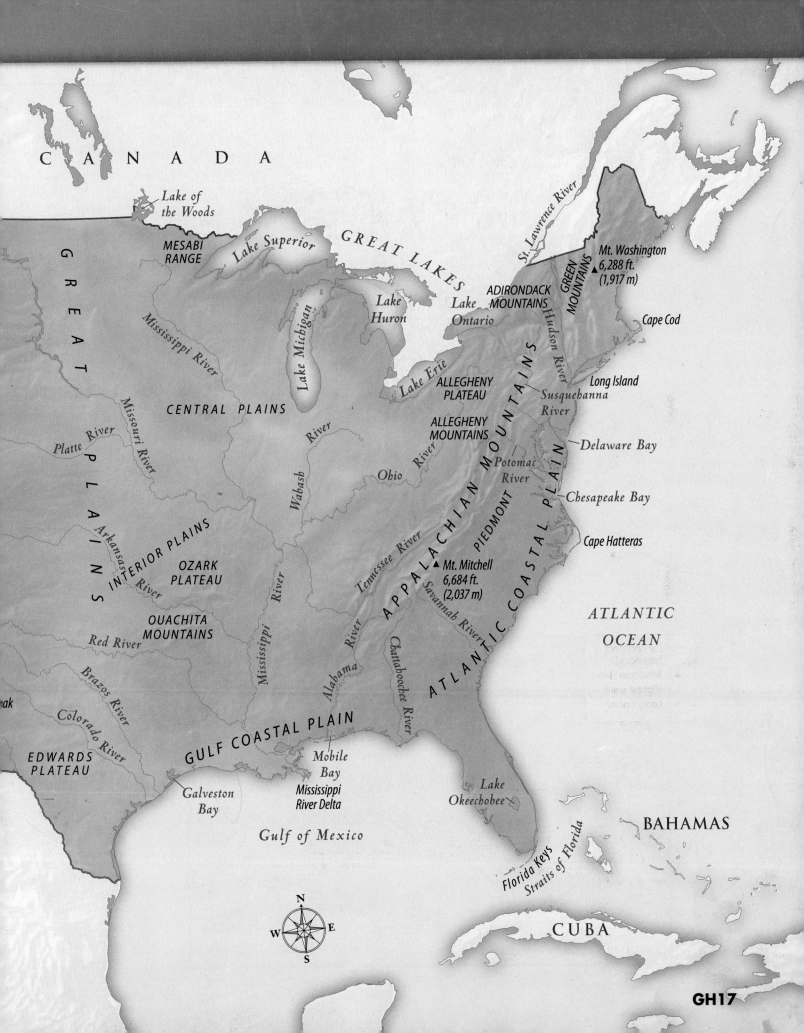

CANADA

Lake of the Woods

MESABI RANGE

Lake Superior

GREAT LAKES

St. Lawrence River

Mt. Washington 6,288 ft. (1,917 m)

GREEN MOUNTAINS

ADIRONDACK MOUNTAINS

Lake Huron

Lake Michigan

Lake Ontario

Lake Erie

Hudson River

Cape Cod

Mississippi River

GREAT PLAINS

CENTRAL PLAINS

ALLEGHENY PLATEAU

ALLEGHENY MOUNTAINS

Susquehanna River

Long Island

Delaware Bay

Missouri River

Platte River

Missouri River

_____ River

Wabash River

Ohio River

Potomac River

APPALACHIAN MOUNTAINS

PIEDMONT

Chesapeake Bay

Cape Hatteras

Arkansas River

INTERIOR PLAINS

OZARK PLATEAU

Mississippi River

Tennessee River

Mt. Mitchell 6,684 ft. (2,037 m)

Savannah River

ATLANTIC OCEAN

Red River

OUACHITA MOUNTAINS

Alabama River

ATLANTIC COASTAL PLAIN

Brazos River

Colorado River

Chattahoochee River

EDWARDS PLATEAU

_eak

GULF COASTAL PLAIN

Mobile Bay

Galveston Bay

Mississippi River Delta

Lake Okeechobee

BAHAMAS

Gulf of Mexico

Florida Keys

Straits of Florida

N
W E
S

CUBA

GH17

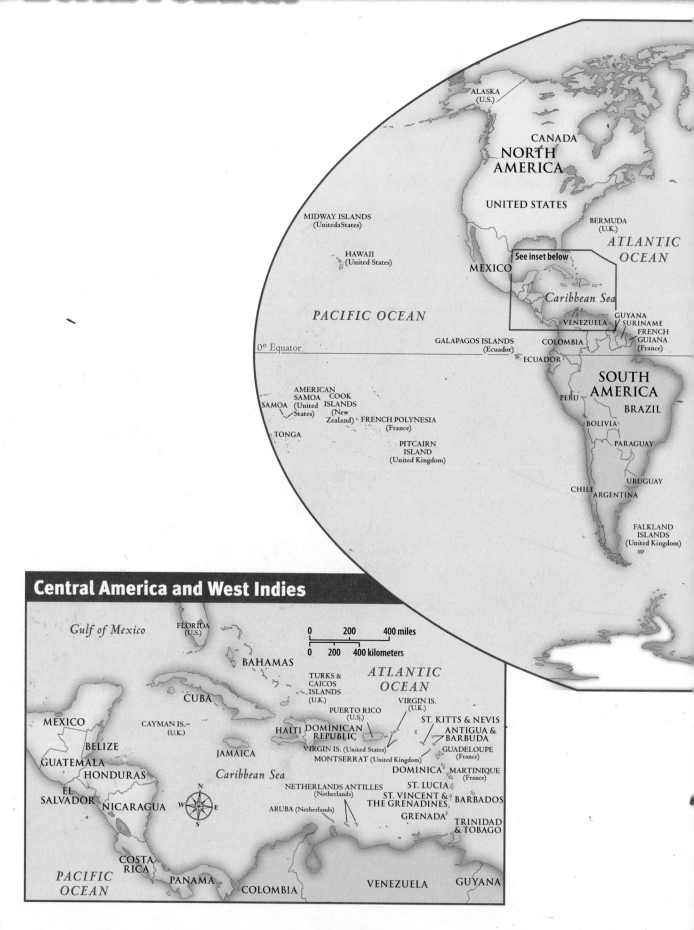

ALASKA
(U.S.)

CANADA

NORTH
AMERICA

UNITED STATES

MIDWAY ISLANDS
(UnitedaStates)

BERMUDA
(U.K.)

*ATLANTIC
OCEAN*

See inset below

HAWAII
(United States)

MEXICO

Caribbean Sea

GUYANA
VENEZUELA   SURINAME
FRENCH
GUIANA
(France)

PACIFIC OCEAN

GALAPAGOS ISLANDS
(Ecuador)

COLOMBIA

0° Equator

ECUADOR

SOUTH
AMERICA

AMERICAN
SAMOA   COOK
SAMOA (United ISLANDS
States)   (New
Zealand) FRENCH POLYNESIA
(France)

PERU

BRAZIL

BOLIVIA

TONGA

PITCAIRN
ISLAND
(United Kingdom)

PARAGUAY

URUGUAY
CHILE
ARGENTINA

FALKLAND
ISLANDS
(United Kingdom)

Central America and West Indies

Gulf of Mexico

FLORIDA
(U.S.)

0   200   400 miles

0   200   400 kilometers

BAHAMAS

TURKS &
CAICOS
ISLANDS
(U.K.)

*ATLANTIC
OCEAN*

CUBA

VIRGIN IS.
(U.K.)

MEXICO

CAYMAN IS.
(U.K.)

PUERTO RICO
(U.S.)

ST. KITTS & NEVIS

HAITI DOMINICAN
REPUBLIC

ANTIGUA &
BARBUDA

BELIZE

VIRGIN IS. (United States)

GUADELOUPE
(France)

GUATEMALA
HONDURAS

JAMAICA

MONTSERRAT (United Kingdom)

DOMINICA MARTINIQUE
(France)

Caribbean Sea

EL
SALVADOR   NICARAGUA

NETHERLANDS ANTILLES
(Netherlands)

ST. LUCIA

ST. VINCENT &
THE GRENADINES BARBADOS

ARUBA (Netherlands)

GRENADA

TRINIDAD
& TOBAGO

COSTA
RICA

*PACIFIC
OCEAN*

PANAMA

COLOMBIA

VENEZUELA

GUYANA

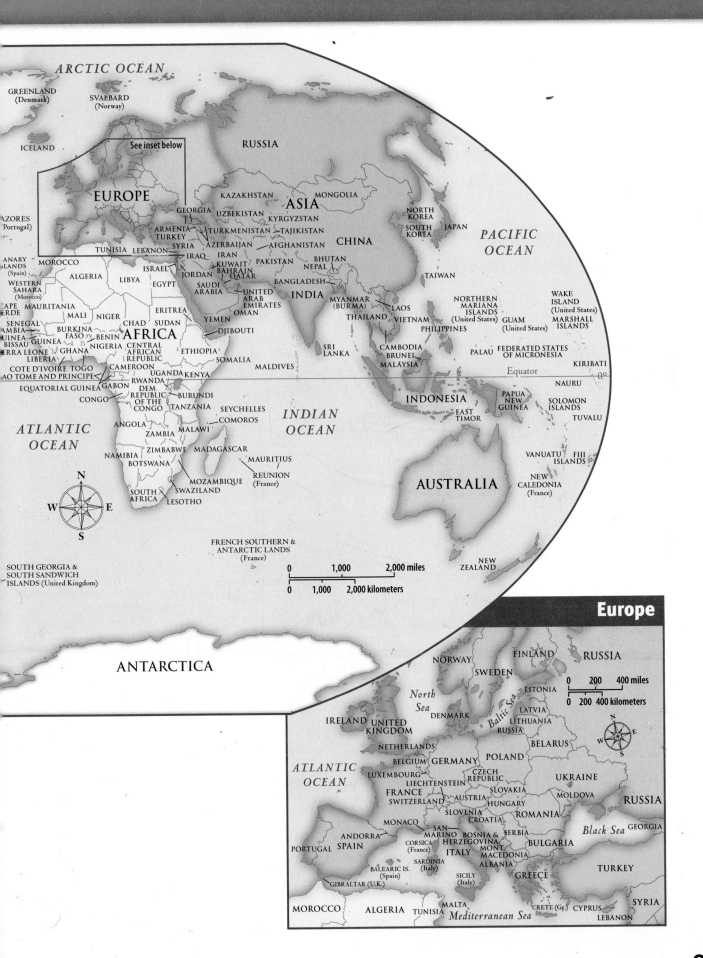

ARCTIC OCEAN

GREENLAND
(Denmark)

SVALBARD
(Norway)

ICELAND

RUSSIA

EUROPE

See inset below

ASIA

KAZAKHSTAN

MONGOLIA

AZORES
(Portugal)

GEORGIA

UZBEKISTAN

KYRGYZSTAN

NORTH
KOREA

ARMENIA
TURKEY

TURKMENISTAN

TAJIKISTAN

SOUTH
KOREA

JAPAN

PACIFIC
OCEAN

CANARY
ISLANDS
(Spain)

MOROCCO

TUNISIA

LEBANON

SYRIA

AZERBAIJAN

AFGHANISTAN

CHINA

IRAQ

IRAN

WESTERN
SAHARA
(Morocco)

ALGERIA

LIBYA

ISRAEL

JORDAN

KUWAIT
BAHRAIN
QATAR

PAKISTAN

NEPAL

BHUTAN

TAIWAN

CAPE
VERDE

MAURITANIA

MALI

NIGER

EGYPT

SAUDI
ARABIA

UNITED
ARAB
EMIRATES

INDIA

BANGLADESH

WAKE
ISLAND
(United States)

NORTHERN
MARIANA
ISLANDS
(United States)

MYANMAR
(BURMA)

OMAN

LAOS

ERITREA

YEMEN

GUAM
(United States)

MARSHALL
ISLANDS

SENEGAL

CHAD

SUDAN

THAILAND

VIETNAM

GAMBIA
GUINEA-
BISSAU

BURKINA
FASO
GUINEA

BENIN

AFRICA

DJIBOUTI

SRI
LANKA

PHILIPPINES

PALAU

FEDERATED STATES
OF MICRONESIA

SIERRA LEONE

GHANA
LIBERIA

NIGERIA

CENTRAL
AFRICAN
REPUBLIC

ETHIOPIA

SOMALIA

MALDIVES

CAMBODIA
BRUNEI
MALAYSIA

KIRIBATI

COTE D'IVOIRE TOGO
SAO TOME AND PRINCIPE

CAMEROON

UGANDA

KENYA

Equator

0°

NAURU

EQUATORIAL GUINEA

GABON

RWANDA

CONGO

DEM.
REPUBLIC
OF THE
CONGO

BURUNDI

TANZANIA

SEYCHELLES

INDIAN
OCEAN

INDONESIA

EAST
TIMOR

PAPUA
NEW
GUINEA

SOLOMON
ISLANDS

TUVALU

ANGOLA

ZAMBIA

MALAWI

COMOROS

ATLANTIC
OCEAN

NAMIBIA

ZIMBABWE

BOTSWANA

MADAGASCAR

MAURITIUS

AUSTRALIA

VANUATU

FIJI
ISLANDS

NEW
CALEDONIA
(France)

N

W   E

S

SOUTH
AFRICA

MOZAMBIQUE
SWAZILAND

LESOTHO

REUNION
(France)

FRENCH SOUTHERN &
ANTARCTIC LANDS
(France)

0   1,000   2,000 miles

0   1,000   2,000 kilometers

NEW
ZEALAND

SOUTH GEORGIA &
SOUTH SANDWICH
ISLANDS (United Kingdom)

ANTARCTICA

Europe

ATLANTIC
OCEAN

NORWAY

SWEDEN

FINLAND

RUSSIA

North
Sea

Baltic Sea

ESTONIA

0   200   400 miles

0   200   400 kilometers

IRELAND

UNITED
KINGDOM

DENMARK

LATVIA

LITHUANIA

RUSSIA

BELARUS

N

W   E

S

NETHERLANDS

BELGIUM

GERMANY

POLAND

LUXEMBOURG

CZECH
REPUBLIC

UKRAINE

FRANCE

LIECHTENSTEIN

SWITZERLAND

AUSTRIA

SLOVAKIA

HUNGARY

SLOVENIA

MOLDOVA

RUSSIA

MONACO

CROATIA

ROMANIA

ANDORRA

SAN
MARINO

BOSNIA &
HERZEGOVINA

SERBIA

Black Sea

GEORGIA

PORTUGAL

SPAIN

CORSICA
(France)

ITALY

MONT.
MACEDONIA

BULGARIA

BALEARIC IS.
(Spain)

SARDINIA
(Italy)

ALBANIA

TURKEY

GIBRALTAR (U.K.)

SICILY
(Italy)

GREECE

MOROCCO

ALGERIA

TUNISIA

MALTA

CRETE (Gr.)

Mediterranean Sea

CYPRUS

SYRIA

LEBANON

GH19

North America: Political

EUROPE

ASIA

ARCTIC OCEAN

North Pole

Chukchi Sea

Bering Sea

Bering Strait

Beaufort Sea

GREENLAND (Denmark)

Baffin Bay

Davis Strait

ALASKA (U.S.)

Fairbanks •

Anchorage •

Nuuk •

Gulf of Alaska

Juneau •

Iqaluit •

Labrador Sea

Yellowknife •

Hudson Bay

CANADA

Newfoundland

Edmonton •

Vancouver •
Seattle •

Winnipeg •

Quebec •

Montreal •
Ottawa ⊛

Boston •

Portland •

Minneapolis •

Toronto •
Detroit •

New York •

ATLANTIC OCEAN

Salt Lake City •

Chicago •

Philadelphia

San Francisco •

Denver •

St. Louis •

Washington, DC ⊛

UNITED STATES

Los Angeles •

Phoenix •

BERMUDA (U.K.)

PACIFIC OCEAN

Dallas •

Atlanta •

Ciudad Juarez •

Houston •

New Orleans •

BAHAMAS

Monterrey •

Miami •

DOMINICAN REPUBLIC

ST. KITTS & NEVIS

Gulf of Mexico

MEXICO

CUBA

PUERTO RICO (U.S.)

ANTIGUA & BARBUDA

DOMINICA

Guadalajara •

HAITI

ST. LUCIA

JAMAICA

BARBADOS

Mexico City ⊛

ST. VINCENT & THE GRENADINES

BELIZE

Caribbean Sea

GRENADA

GUATEMALA

HONDURAS

TRINIDAD & TOBAGO

EL SALVADOR

NICARAGUA

PANAMA

COSTA RICA

SOUTH AMERICA

—— International boundary

⊛ National capital

• Other city

N
W E
S

0 300 600 miles

0 300 600 kilometers

North America: Physical

EUROPE

ASIA

ARCTIC OCEAN

Greenland Sea

Lincoln Sea

Greenland

Baffin Bay

Point Barrow

Beaufort Sea

Bering Strait

BROOKS RANGE

Mt. McKinley
20,320 ft.
(6,194 m) ▲

Yukon R.

ALASKA RANGE

YUKON PLATEAU

Mt. Logan
19,551 ft.
(5,959 m) ▲

Mackenzie R.

Davis Strait

Cape Farewell

Hudson Bay

CANADIAN SHIELD

Peace R.

Churchill R.

Saskatchewan R.

Lake Winnipeg

Newfoundland

Gulf of St. Lawrence

Vancouver Island

R O C K Y

Snake R.

COAST MOUNTAINS

Missouri River

Great Lakes

Gulf of Maine
Cape Cod

COAST RANGES

M O U N T A I N S

Obio R.

APPALACHIAN MOUNTAINS

Long Island

ATLANTIC OCEAN

PACIFIC OCEAN

GREAT BASIN

G R E A T

Colorado R.

Mt. Whitney
14,494 ft. (4,418 m) ▲

Death Valley
-282 ft. (-86 m)

SONORAN DESERT

P L A I N S

OZARK PLATEAU

Mississippi R.

Red R.

Chesapeake Bay

Cape Hatteras

Bermuda (U.K.)

BAJA CALIFORNIA

Rio Grande

SIERRA MADRE OCCIDENTAL

SIERRA MADRE ORIENTAL

C O A S T A L   P L A I N

Gulf of Mexico

W E S T   I N D I E S

Gulf of California

Orizaba
18,855 ft.
(5,747 m) ▲

YUCATAN PENINSULA

Puerto Rico (U.S.)

Caribbean Sea

—— International boundary
⊗ National capital
▲ Mountain peak

Lake Nicaragua

Isthmus of Panama

SOUTH AMERICA

CENTRAL AMERICA

N
W   E
S

| 0 | 300 | 600 miles |
| 0 | 300 | 600 kilometers |

GH21

South America: Political

NORTH AMERICA

Caribbean Sea

Barranquilla

Maracaibo
Valencia ⊛ Caracas

VENEZUELA

Georgetown
GUYANA Paramaribo
Cayenne
SURINAME
FRENCH GUIANA (France)

ATLANTIC OCEAN

Medellin
Bogota
Cali
COLOMBIA

Quito ⊛
ECUADOR
Guayaquil
Iquitos

GALAPAGOS ISLANDS (Ecuador)

Manaus
Belem

PERU

Trujillo

Recife

BRAZIL

Callao Lima
Cuzco

Salvador (Bahia)

Arequipa
La Paz
BOLIVIA
Sucre

Brasilia ⊛

Belo Horizonte

PARAGUAY

Rio de Janeiro

Antofagasta

Asuncion ⊛

Sao Paulo

Tucuman

CHILE

Porto Alegre

Cordoba
Rosario

Valparaiso
Santiago ⊛

URUGUAY
Montevideo ⊛

Buenos Aires

Concepcion

ARGENTINA

PACIFIC OCEAN

ATLANTIC OCEAN

— International boundary
⊛ National capital
• Other city

0   400   800 miles
0   400   800 kilometers

FALKLAND ISLANDS (ISLAS MALVINAS) (U.K.)

Punta Arenas

SOUTH GEORGIA (U.K.)

South America: Physical

NORTH
AMERICA

Caribbean Sea

Orinoco R.

VENEZUELA

GUYANA

FRENCH
GUIANA
(France)

COLOMBIA

SURINAME

GUIANA HIGHLANDS

Negro River

ECUADOR

Amazon River

*Galapagos
Islands
(Ecuador)*

*AMAZON
BASIN*

Tapajos River

Xingu River

PERU

Madeira River

BRAZIL

Tocantins River

Sao Francisco River

ANDES

*Lake
Titicaca*

*BRAZILIAN
HIGHLANDS*

BOLIVIA

Paraguay R.

River

MOUNTAINS

*ATACAMA
DESERT*

PARAGUAY

Parana

Mt. Ojos del Salado
22,572 ft. (6,880 m)

ANDES MOUNTAINS

River

CHILE

Parana

Mt. Aconcagua ▲
22,834 ft. (6,960 m)

URUGUAY

PACIFIC
OCEAN

Parana

ARGENTINA

Rio de la Plata

PAMPAS

ATLANTIC
OCEAN

ATLANTIC
OCEAN

— International boundary
▲ Mountain peak

PATAGONIA

| 0 | 400 | 800 miles |

| 0 | 400 | 800 kilometers |

*Falkland Islands
(Islas Malvinas)
(U.K.)*

*Strait of
Magellan*

TIERRA DEL FUEGO

Cape
Horn

*South Georgia
(U.K.)*

The 50 United States

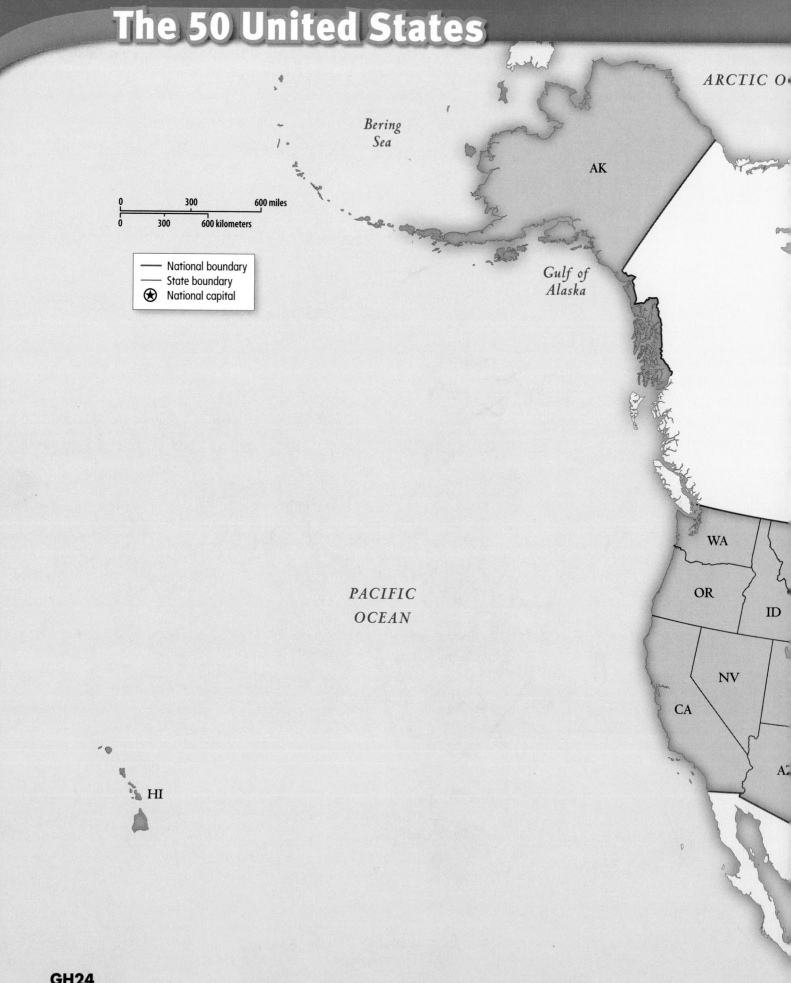

ARCTIC O...

Bering
Sea

AK

Gulf of
Alaska

0   300   600 miles
0   300   600 kilometers

—— National boundary
— State boundary
⊛ National capital

PACIFIC

OCEAN

WA

OR

ID

NV

CA

AZ

HI

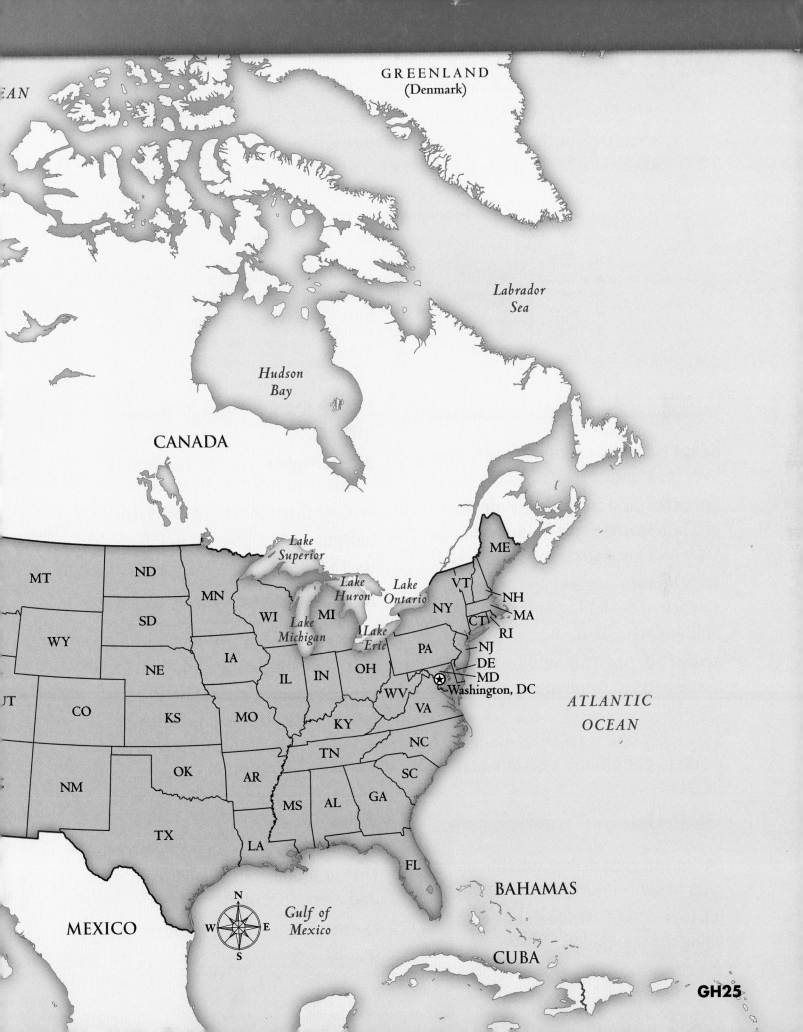

GREENLAND
(Denmark)

EAN

Labrador
Sea

Hudson
Bay

CANADA

Lake
Superior

MT   ND
                        ME
        MN   Lake   VT
    SD   Lake Huron Lake   NH
WI   Ontario NY   MA
WY   MI   CT
        Lake   RI
IA   Michigan Lake   NJ
NE   IL IN Erie PA DE
CO   OH   MD
        WV   Washington, DC
UT   KS MO   VA   ATLANTIC
                        OCEAN
NM OK KY
        AR TN NC
            SC
        MS AL GA
TX
    LA   FL
                    BAHAMAS
MEXICO   N
        W   E Gulf of
            Mexico
        S   CUBA

GH25

Glossary

The Glossary will help you to pronounce and understand the meanings of the vocabulary terms in this book. The page number at the end of the definition tells where the term first appears.

Pronunciation Key

a	at	ī	ice	u	up	th	thin
ā	ape	î	pierce	ū	use	th	this
ä	far	o	hot	ü	rule	zh	measure
âr	care	ō	old	ů	pull	ə	about, taken,
e	end	ô	fork	ûr	turn		pencil, lemon,
ē	me	oi	oil	hw	white		circus
i	it	ou	out	ng	song		

A

adapt (ə dapt′) To change the way you live. (p. 19)

ancestor (an′ ses tər) An early member of a family who came before you, such as a great-grandparent. (p. 133)

architecture (är′ ki tek′chər) The art or science of designing and making buildings. (p. 110)

artifact (är′ ti fakt) Something that was made or used by people in the past. (p. 53)

assembly line (ə sem′ blē līn) A line of workers performing a certain task. (p. 91)

B

bar graph (bär graf) A graph that uses bars to show information. (p. 84)

barter (bär′ tər) To trade things without using money. (p. 53)

bill (bil) A written idea for a law. (p. 231)

Bill of Rights (bil uv rīts) The first ten changes to the Constitution that protect the rights of citizens. (p. 223)

budget (buj′it) A plan for using money. (p. 157)

C

capital (kap′i təl) A city where a country or a state has its government. (p. 6)

capital resource (kap′i təl rē′ sôrs) The tools, machines, and factories people use to produce goods. (p. 165)

capitol (kap′ i təl) The building in which the state or national government meets. (p. 207)

cardinal directions (kär′də nal di rek′shəns) The directions north, east, south, and west. (p. 10)

century (sen′chərē) One hundred years. (p. 68)

citizen (sit′i zən) A person who is a member of a community, state, or country. (p. 197)

colony (kol′ə nē) A place that is ruled by another country. (p. 61)

common good (kom′ən gůd) What is best for the most people. (p. 222)

community (kə mū′ ni tē) A place where people live, work, and play. (p. 5)

commute (kə mūt′) To travel a distance to and from work. (p. 16)

constitution (kän stə tü′ shən) A written plan of government. (p. 66)

consumer (kən sü′ mər) A person who buys a good or uses a service. (p. 150)

cooperate (kō äpə rāt) To work together. (p. 186)

council (sit′i koun′səl) The branch of local government that makes laws. (p. 216)

culture (kul′ chər) A way of life shared by a group of people. (p. 53)

custom (kus′təm) A way of doing something that is shared by many people. (p. 103)

D

dam (dam) A wall built across a stream or river that holds back and controls the water. (p. 37)

decade (dek′ ād) Ten years. (p. 68)

degree (di grē′) A unit of measuring distance on Earth's surface. (p. 138)

demand (di mand′) The number of people who want certain goods or sevices. (p. 168)

discrimination (di skrim′i nā′ shən) An unfair difference in the way people are treated. (p. 83)

diverse (di vûrs) Not all the same. (p. 109)

domestic trade (də mes′ tik trād) Trade that takes place within the borders of a country. (p. 184)

E

economy (i kon′ə mē) The way a place uses its money, goods, natural resources, and services. (p. 152)

ecosystem (ē′ kō sis′ təm) A community of living and nonliving things in a certain area. (p. 40)

elevator (el′ə vā tər) A machine that moves people and things up and down in a building. (p. 89)

employee (em ploi′ ē) Someone who gets paid to work for a person or a business. (p. 149)

environment (en vī′ rən mənt) The air, water, land, and other things that surround animals, people, and plants. (p. 32)

equator (i kwā′tər) An imaginary line around Earth halfway between the North Pole and the South Pole. (p. 76)

ethnic group (eth' nik grüp) A group of people that shares the same language and culture. (p. 109)

executive branch (eg zek'ū tiv branch) The part of government that carries out laws. (p. 198)

expense (ek spens') Something people spend money on to buy or to do. (p. 157)

explorer (ek splôr' ər) A person who goes to a new place to find out about it. (p. 71)

export (ek spôrt') To send goods out of a country to be sold. (p. 179)

F

factory (fak'tə rē) A place where things are manufactured. (p. 173)

festival (fes'tə vəl) A celebration. (p. 7)

flow chart (flō chärt) A chart that shows the different steps necessary to complete a process. (p. 204)

founder (found' er) A person who starts something, such as a business or a town. (p. 125)

frontier (frun tîr) The far edge of a country where new people are just beginning to settle. (p. 71)

G

generation (jen'ə rā shn) A group of people born and living around the same time. (p. 103)

geography (jē og'rə fē) The study of Earth and the way people and animals live on it. (p. 5)

governor (guv'ər nər) The person elected to be in charge of the state government. (p. 207)

graph (graf) A drawing that shows information, such as the relationship between two things. (p. 84)

grid (grid) Lines that cross each other on a map. (p. 138)

H

hemisphere (hem' is fîr) One half of Earth or another sphere. (p. 76)

heritage (her'i tij) Something handed down from the past. (p. 103)

hero (hîr ō) Someone you respect because of his or her achievements or personal qualities. (p. 117)

holiday (hol' i dā) A day on which people or events are honored and celebrated. (p. 130)

human resource (hyü mən rē sôrs) A person who works for a business. (p. 165)

I

immigrant (im'i grənt) A person who comes from one country to live in another. (p. 80)

import (im pôrt') To bring in goods made or grown in another country. (p. 178)

income (in' kum) Money someone receives for working. (p. 157)

industry (in' də strē) A special type of business that makes things or provides a service. (p. 79)

intermediate directions (in tər mēd'dē it di rek'shəns) A direction halfway between two cardinal directions. (p. 10)

international trade (in tər nash'ə nəl trād) Trade between different countries. (p. 182)

interstate highway (in tər stāt hī'wā') A road that connects two or more states. (p. 212)

━━━━━ J ━━━━━

judicial branch (jü dish' əl branch) The part of government that decides if laws are fair and follow the Constitution. (p. 199)

jury (jür'ē) A group of citizens chosen to hear the facts in a case that has been brought before a court of law, and to make a decision based on the facts and the law. (p. 222)

━━━━━ L ━━━━━

landform (land' fôrm) The shapes of Earth's surface. (p. 19)

latitude (lat' i tüd) A measure of distance north or south of the equator. (p. 138)

legislative branch (lej'is lā tiv branch) The part of government that writes and passes laws. (p. 199)

levee (le' vē) A long wall made of dirt or concrete built next to a river or a lake to prevent flooding. (p. 39)

line graph (līn graf) A graph that shows information that changes over time. (p. 170)

local government (lō'kəl guv'ərn mənt) A group of people who run a town or city. (p. 215)

longitude (lon' ji tüd) A measure of distance east or west of the prime meridian. (p. 138)

━━━━━ M ━━━━━

manufacture (man yə fak' chər) To make a product using machines, often in large amounts. (p. 91)

map scale (map skāl) The measurement a map uses to show the real distance between places on Earth. (p. 26)

mayor (mā'ər) The head of a local government. (p. 215)

migration (mī grā' shən) Movement from one part of the country to another. (p. 82)

mineral (min'ər əl) A natural resource that is not a plant or an animal. (p. 29)

━━━━━ N ━━━━━

natural resource (nach'ər əl rē' sôrs) A material found in nature that people use. (p. 23)

nonprofit (non prof'it) Something that does not make money. (p. 230)

nonrenewable resource (non ri nü' ə bəl rē'sôrs) A natural resource that cannot be replaced. (p. 30)

O

opportunity cost (op' ər tü' ni tē kôst) The value of the next best choice when you choose one thing instead of another. (p. 161)

P

Patriot (pā'trē ət) A colonist who supported independence. (p. 65)

pioneer (pī' nîr') The first of a group of people to settle in an area. (p. 71)

plain (plān) An area of flat or almost flat land. (p. 20)

plateau (pla tō') An area of flat land higher than the land around it. (p. 21)

primary source (prī' mer ē sôrs) A firsthand account of events. (pp. 74, 105, 158, 202)

prime meridian (prīm mə rid' ē ən) An imaginary line that runs from the North Pole to the South Pole through Greenwich, England. (p. 76)

producer (pro dü' sər) Someone who makes, grows, or supplies goods or services. (p. 150)

profit (prof'it) The money a business makes after paying for tools, employees, and other costs. (p. 151)

R

recycle (rē sī' kəl) To reuse a product and turn it into something that can be used again. (p. 34)

region (rē jen) An area with common features that set it apart from other areas. (p. 20)

reservoir (rez'ər vwär) A place to store water. (p. 37)

revolution (rev' ə lü' shən) A fight that often leads to the end of one government and the beginning of a new one. (p. 65)

road map (rōd map) A map that shows roads. (p. 212)

rural (rüe'əl) Of or about an area that is far from a city and has farms or open country. (p. 15)

S

savings account (sā vingz ə kaunt) Money a person keeps in a bank that pays interest. (p. 162)

scarcity (skâr' si tē) A shortage of goods and services that are available. (p. 168)

settler (set' lər) A person who moves to find land. (p. 56)

skyscraper (skī'skrā pər) A very tall building. (p. 89)

slavery (slā' və rē) Forcing people to work without pay and without freedom. (p. 59)

sovereign (sov′ ərin) Independent; not controlled by others. (p. 219)

specialize (spesh′ə līz) To make one thing very well. (p. 176)

sphere (sfîr) A round object like a ball. (p. 76)

state highway (stāt hī′wā′) A road that begins and finishes inside a state. (p. 212)

suburb (sub′ûrb) A community near a large city. (p. 14)

supply (sə plī′) The amount of goods or services that are available. (p. 168)

T

tax (taks) Money paid to a government for services. (p. 62)

territory (ter′i tôr′ē) An area of land owned by a country. (p. 72)

time line (tīm līn) A list that tells the order of important events. (p. 68)

tradition (trə dish′ ən) A custom handed down from the past . (p. 133)

transcontinental (trans kon tə nen′təl) Crossing an entire continent. (p. 87)

transportation (trans pər tā′shən) A way of getting from one place to another. (p. 16)

U

urban (ûr′bən) Relating to a city and its surrounding communties. (p. 13)

V

value (val′ yū) An idea that people in a culture care about and think is important. (p. 117)

volunteer (vol′ ən tîr′) A person who chooses to do something without getting paid. (p. 229)

Y

year (yîr) Any period of 12 months. (p. 68)

Index

This index lists many topics that appear in the book, along with the pages on which they are found. Page numbers after an *m* refer you to a map.

Index

Index

Credits

Museum of Modern Art/Licensed by SCALA ; © ARS, NY/Art Resource, NY. 111: (b) Dynamic Graphics /JupiterImages; (t) Lindsay Hebberd/CORBIS. 112: (b) Frank Driggs Collection/Hulton Archive/Getty Images; (t) Eliot Elisofon/Time Life Pictures/Getty Images. 113: (b) James Nesterwitz/Alamy Images; (t) The Granger Collection, New York. 114: (bl) David Young-Wolff/PhotoEdit; (br) Dynamic Graphics/JupiterImages; (tr) David M. Grossman/The Image Works, Inc. 115: (bl) MMH; (tl) MMH; (tr) MMH. 116: (bcr) Andre Jenny/Alamy Images; (bl) Marilyn "Angel" Wynn/Nativestock Pictures. 116-117: Brand X Pictures/PunchStock. 117: (b) Marilyn "Angel" Wynn/Nativestock Pictures. 120: (b) Andre Jenny/Alamy Images. 123: (b) Andre Jenny/Alamy Images. 124: (bcl) Kristine Ambrosen; (bcr) Dinodia Photo Library; (bl) Amanda Stratford/The Hannibal Courier-Post; (br) Deborah Davis/PhotoEdit. 124-125: Randall Hyman. 125: (b) Amanda Stratford/The Hannibal Courier-Post. 126: (b) Getty Images; (t) Kristine Ambrosen. 127: (b) Cheron Bayna/Image Courtesy of Pat Mora. 128: (b) Blend Images/Alamy Images; (t) Jeff Hunter/Getty Images. 129: (b) Dinodia Photo Library; (t) Xinhua/Landov. 130: (bl) Bob Daemmrich/Bob Daemmrich Photography; (br) Bob Daemmrich/Bob Daemmrich Photography; (t) Larry Kolvoor/Austin Am-Statesman/WPN. 131: (b) Jeff Hunter/Getty Images; (t) Deborah Davis/PhotoEdit. 132: (bc) ImageState/Alamy Images; (bl) Anders Ryman/CORBIS; (br) David Muscroft/Alamy Images. 132-133: Craig Pershouse/Lonely Planet Images. 133: (b) Anders Ryman/CORBIS. 134: (b) Jon Arnold/Danita Delimont Stock Photography; (t) Marcus Brooke/Getty Images. 134-135: (b) ImageState/Alamy Images. 135: (t) Rodolfo Arpia/Alamy Images. 136: (b) Adams Picture Library/Alamy Images; (br) David Muscroft/Alamy Images; (tl) SCPhotos/Alamy Images. 137: (b) Marcus Brooke/Getty Images; (t) Arco Images/Alamy Images. 139: (b) Sergio Pitamitz/Danita Delimont Stock Photography. 140: (b) Ken Karp for MMH; (t) Peter Byron/PhotoEdit. 144: (t) MMH.

145: James Lauritz/Digital Vision/Getty Images. 146: (b) New Orleans Crafts Guild, Inc.; (tl) New Orleans Crafts Guild, Inc.; (tr) Steve Hamblin/Alamy Images. 147: (b) Bettmann/CORBIS; (tl) The Granger Collection, New York; (tr) Dennis MacDonald/Alamy Images. 148: (bcr) Comstock Images/PunchStock; (bl) Jose Luis Pelaez, Inc./CORBIS. 148-149: Gibson Stock Photography. 149: (br) Jose Luis Pelaez, Inc./CORBIS. 152: (br) Ambient Images Inc./Alamy Images; (tl) Comstock Images/PunchStock. 153: (bc) Chris Hammond/Alamy Images; (bl) Kitt Cooper-Smith/Alamy Images; (br) © Smithsonian Institution, National Numismatic Collection; (c) MMH; (tr) Zedcor Wholly Owned/Jupiterimages. 155: (bl) Ken Karp for MMH; (br) Ambient Images Inc./Alamy Images. 156: (bcl) Marc Romanelli/Jupiterimages; (bl) Cindy Charles/PhotoEdit. 156-157: James Darell/Photodisc/Getty Images. 157: (br) Cindy Charles/PhotoEdit. 158: (b) AP Photos; (bl) MMH; (t) Michael Geissinger/The Image Works, Inc. 159: (t) Marc Romanelli/Jupiterimages. 161: (bl) Gabe Palmer/Alamy Images; (br) Tomi/PhotoLink/Photodisc/Getty Images; (tr) Stockdisc/PunchStock. 162: (b) James Darell/Photodisc/Getty Images. 163: (bl) MMH; (br) MMH; (tl) MMH. 164: (bc) David Frazier/CORBIS; (bl) Joeseph Sohm-Visions of America/Getty Images; (br) James Schwabel/Panoramic Images. 164-165: Peter Beck/CORBIS. 165: (br) Joeseph Sohm-Visions of America/Getty Images. 166: (c) isifa Image Service s.r.o./Alamy Images; (tl) Syracuse Newspapers / David Lassman/The Image Works, Inc.; (tr) Harald Theissen/Alamy Images. 167: (br) George Contorakes/Masterfile; (cl) David Frazier/CORBIS; (cr) Bill Barksdale/AgStockUSA; (tc) Lynn Stone/AgStockUSA. 168: (br) Paul Sakuma/AP Images. 168-169: (b) James Schwabel/Panoramic Images. 169: (b) isifa Image Service s.r.o./Alamy Images; (tr) Feldman & Associates. 170-171: (bkgd) Richard Price/Getty Images. 172: (bcl) CORBIS; (bcr) Ancient Art & Architecture/Danita Delimont Stock Photography; (bl) AFP/Getty Images; (br) William Caram/CORBIS. 172-173: David R. Frazier Photolibrary, Inc/Alamy Images. 173: (b) AFP/Getty Images. 174: (tl) The Granger Collection, New York; (tr) CORBIS. 175: (tl) Bruce Dale/National Geographic/Getty Images; (tr) © 2006 Stratus Imaging. 176: (b) David Buffington/Photodisc/Getty Images; (cb)

Dave G. Houser/CORBIS; (ct) Erik Simonsen/Transtock Inc./Alamy Images; (t) Stockbyte/Getty Images. 177: (bl) J Marshall - Tribaleye Images/Alamy Images; (br) Siede Preis/Photodisc/Getty Images; (c) Ancient Art & Architecture/Danita Delimont Stock Photography; (tcl) Brand X Pictures/Alamy Images; (tcr) Matthew Ward/Dorling Kindersley/Getty Images; (tl) Hugh Threlfall/Alamy Images; (tr) Nikreates/Alamy Images. 178: (b) MMH; (tl) Nature Picture Library/Alamy Images. 179: (b) J Marshall - Tribaleye Images/Alamy Images; (t) William Caram/CORBIS. 180: (bcr) MMH; (bl) Tina Manley/Alamy Images; (br) Elyse Lewin/Getty Images. 180-181: NASA Human Space Flight Gallery. 181: (b) Tina Manley/Alamy Images. 182: (br) Getty Images. 184: (bl) MMH; (br) Amanda J. Freeman/RR Donnelly/MMH. 185: (b) MMH; (t) Jeff Cadge/Getty Images. 186: (b) Steve Barsky; (tc) AP Photos; (tl) Elyse Lewin/Getty Images; (tr) Art Kowalsky/Alamy Images. 187: (tcl) BennettPhoto/Alamy Images; (tcr) Kristi J. Black/CORBIS; (tl) Andrew Ward/Life File/Getty Images; (tr) Dallas and John Heaton/Free Agents Limited/CORBIS. 188: (b) Ken Karp for MMH; (t) David R. Frazier Photolibrary, Inc./Alamy Images. 189: (b) MMH. 192: (t) Ken Karp for MMH.

193: Wally McNamee/CORBIS; (t) Photodisc/Getty Images. 194: (b) The Granger Collection, New York; (tc) Bettmann/CORBIS; (tl) Bettmann/CORBIS; (tr) Andre Jenny/Alamy Images. 195: (b) Phil Schermeister/CORBIS; (tl) Sarina Wilder/Wells Memorial School; (tr) Richard Klune/CORBIS. 196: (bcl) Dean Fox/SuperStock; (b) Evan Vucci/AP Photos; (br) Pete Saloutos/CORBIS. 196-197: Bill Brooks/Alamy Images. 197: (b) Evan Vucci/AP Photos. 198: (t) Dennis O'Clair/Getty Images. 199: (tl) Dean Fox/SuperStock; (tr) Hisham F. Ibrahim/Photodisc/Getty Images. 202: (bl) Steve Allen/Brand X/CORBIS; (br) Comstock/Jupiterimages; (cl) MMH. 203: (b) Dennis O'Clair/Getty Images; (tl) age fotostock/SuperStock; (tr) Pete Saloutos/CORBIS. 206: (bc) Ryan McVay/Getty Images; (bl) John Elk III Photography; (br) John Miller/AP Photos. 206-207: Bob Daemmrich/CORBIS. 207: (b) John Elk III Photography. 208: (b) Digital Vision/PunchStock; (t) Ryan McVay/Getty Images. 210: (bc) Courtesy of the Arizona Department of Public Safety; (t) David Schmidt/Masterfile. 211: (b) Bob Daemmrich/CORBIS; (t) John Miller/AP Photos. 213: (br) Peter Horree/Alamy Images. 214: (bl) Peter Steiner/Alamy Images; (br) Paul J. Richards/AFP/Getty Images. 214-215: Philip Rostron/Masterfile. 215: (b) Peter Steiner/Alamy Images. 218: (b) Peter Mundy/Alamy Images; (cr) Doug Pearson/Jon Arnold Images/Alamy Images. 219: (t) Paul J. Richards/AFP/Getty Images. 220: (bcr) Jonathan Ernst/Reuters/CORBIS; (bl) Jeff Cadge/Getty Images; (br) Jerry Jacka, 2006. 220-221: George Shelley/Masterfile. 221: (b) Jeff Cadge/Getty Images. 222: (tc) Tony Freeman/PhotoEdit. 223: (b) Flip Schulke/CORBIS; (t) Jason Reed/Reuters/Landov. 224: (b) Jonathan Ernst/Reuters/CORBIS. 225: (t) Rick Scuteri/AP Photos. 226: (b) Jason Reed/Reuters/Landov; (t) Jerry Jacka, 2006. 227: (b) Bonnie Kamin/PhotoEdit. 228: (bcl) Billy Hustace/Getty Images; (bcr) David Ashley/CORBIS; (bl) Youth Service America 2007; (br) Bob Daemmrich/PhotoEdit. 228-229: Jeffry Myers/Index Stock Imagery. 229: (b) Youth Service America 2007. 230: (b) Erik S. Lesser/Getty Images; (bl) Billy Hustace/Getty Images; (t) Jennifer Hearn. 231: (c) Siede Preis/Photodisc; (tr) Bob Lapree/Union Leader Corporation. 232: (b) David Ashley/CORBIS; (t) U.S. Senate Photographic Studio. 233: (b) Steve Jaffe/Reuters/CORBIS; (t) Tom & Dee Ann McCarthy/CORBIS. 234: (tl) The Granger Collection, New York; (tr) The Granger Collection, New York. 235: (b) Erik S. Lesser/Getty Images; (tl) The Granger Collection, New York; (tr) Bob Daemmrich/PhotoEdit. 236: (b) MMH; (t) Visions of America, LLC/Alamy Images. 240: (t) MMH.

R3: (b) Chuck Savage/CORBIS. R7: (b) Amanda Stratford/The Hannibal Courier-Post. R8: (c) Stockdisc/PunchStock. R9: (b) Cindy Charles/PhotoEdit. R11: (c) Pete Saloutos/CORBIS. GH4: (b) Ed Boettcher/CORBIS; (t) Dennis O'Clair/Getty Images. GH5: (b) Aerial/Terrestrial Photography; (c) Steve Allen/Getty Images; (t) F. Schussler/PhotoLink/Getty Images. GH8: (l) Bryan Allen/CORBIS; (r) MMH.

ACKNOWLEDGMENTS

Grateful acknowledgment is given to the following authors and publishers. Every effort has been made to trace the ownership of all copyrighted material and to secure the necessary permissions to reprint these selections. In the case of some selections for which acknowledgment is not given, extensive research has failed to locate the copyright holders.

"... there emerges..." Institute of Noetic Sciences brochure, 1973. Reprinted by permission of the Institute of Noetic Sciences.

"Paul Bunyan, the Mightiest Logger of Them All" from American Tall Tales by Mary Pope Osborn, copyright © 1991 by Mary Pope Osborn. Alfred A. Knopf

from "House supports making the pumpkin the state fruit" by Anne Saunders. Copyright March 8, 2006, Associated Press.